Ricky Tomlinson is one of Britain's best-loved actors and entertainers. Famous as the irascible sofa slob Jim Royle of *The Royle Family*, he has also scored as the crackpot football manager Mike Bassett, and has starred in a procession of television shows including *Brookside*, *Cracker* and *Down to Earth*.

His many film appearances take in such movies as *The 51st State*, *Riff Raff* and *Raining Stones*. He was voted Best Comedy Actor for his performance as Jim Royle, and both his autobiography, *Ricky* and *Football My Arse!* were bestselling books.

Ricky was born in September 1939. He was brought up in Liverpool, where he still lives with his wife Rita.

FOOTBALL MY ARSE!

Ricky Tomlinson

SPHERE

First published in Great Britain in 2005 by Time Warner Books
This paperback edition published in 2006 by Time Warner Books
Reprinted by Sphere in 2006, 2007, 2009

A CIP catalogue for this title is available from the British Library

ISBN 978 0 7515 3735 2

Papers used by Sphere are natural, renewable and
recyclable products sourced from well-managed forests
and certified in accordance with the rules of the
Forest Stewardship Council.

Mixed Sources
Product group from well-managed
forests and other controlled sources
www.fsc.org   Cert no. SGS-COC-004081
© 1996 Forest Stewardship Council
FSC

Typeset in Melior by M Rules
Printed and bound in Great Britain by
Clays Ltd, St Ives plc

Sphere
An imprint of
Little, Brown Book Group
100 Victoria Embankment
London EC4Y 0DY

An Hachette UK Company
www.hachette.co.uk

www.littlebrown.co.uk

To Rita and Eileen
What a pair of sweepers!

Acknowledgements

I wish to thank the Sphere team, and in particular Antonia Hodgson, for their expert help in getting this book into the net. I am indebted to Ian Allen, Mike Harkin and Michael Giller for their safety-net checking work on the hundreds of football anecdotes that have been knitted together to make *Football My Arse!* Thanks to Peter Cotton for a perfectly tailored jacket, to Marie Hrynczak for the design and production, to Tamsyn Berryman and Philip Parr for their editorial support and to Ian Blackwell and Vito Ingelese at Popperfoto for their help with picture research. Most of all, thanks to all my pals in and around the game who have so willingly helped me dig out the stories. You are too many to mention, but you know who you are! And, of course, thanks to my pal, sports historian Norman Giller, for his diligent guidance, and to Rita for being there. I suppose I also have to thank (this is sounding like an Oscar acceptance speech) Mike Bassett for his introduction, but as he is taking half my money why the bloody hell should I? My special thanks to Mike Bassett creators Rob Sprackling and John R. Smith for letting him loose on the introduction. Cheers, the laugh's on me.

Contents

Introduction by Mike Bassett

I've been a close personal friend of Ricky Tomlinson for many years – any closer and we would have been consenting adults. We look extremely similar, and if ever they are going to film my life Ricky would be my ideal choice – after Tom Selleck. I like to think we both embody that traditional British virtue of stiff upper lip – though that could be the lacquer on my moustache. I first met him when he captained a celebrity eleven against my England team. We lost 4–3 to a late winner from Kavanagh QC, who asked some serious questions of our defence.

As I recall Ricky was no mean footballer himself. In fact, he was extremely generous, giving away one free-kick after another. I was there for all his games and can safely say he well earned his nickname Cinderella . . . because he was always late for the ball. His dribbling skills were second only to George Best's after sixteen pints of lager and he had a tendency to sit deeper than Dawn French.

I feel the publishers would have been wiser to commission me to write this book, because they would have got the full inside story on the England dressing-room. Not just the tittle and the tattle but the full Monty, too. Who else, for instance, could compare the sizes of David Beckham and Sol Campbell? Well, I can let you into a secret . . . Becks wears size-nine boots and Campbell size tens. What did you think I was talking about? The size of their England caps?

Ricky's acting is even better than some of the stuff you see on the football pitch – and I'm including the German high-tariff divers in this! There can be no higher compliment than that. So when Ricky asked me if I would write a foreword for his new book I was thrilled – particularly when he mentioned the fee.

I have to be fair and admit that Ricky – or Rickety, as Ken Dodd calls him – has collated an astonishing anthology of footballing anecdotes. Ricky tells them all with his usual comic genius. You could say he's got a nose for a good story. He has called on his many friends and contacts in the game to help him tell amazing tales of the unexpected, quite a few of them being revealed for the very first time. His mate Norman Giller, a know-all sports historian, has been particularly helpful in polishing and pruning the stories.

If you are any sort of a football fan – or even if you don't know an overlap from an underpass – you will find this a fascinating as well as an extremely funny book.

Mind you, Ricky hasn't included my favourite Jimmy Greaves story. When he was playing for England against Brazil in the 1962 World Cup quarter-finals in Chile, Greavsie caught hold of a stray dog that had run on to the pitch. As he picked up the dog and carried it to the touchline, Jimmy felt a warm sensation. The dog had pissed all the way down his England shirt and shorts. You could say the dog was relieved. 'I got pissed a few times in those days, and I often got pissed off with being kicked and hacked,' Greavsie told me. 'But this was the first and only time that I got pissed on!' Garrincha, the legendary Brazilian winger, claimed the dog after the match, took it home with him and called it 'Jimmy'. He should have given it the full name of Jimmy Riddle!

That's one story that Ricky missed, but, as you are about to find out, he has dug out hundreds of others as he proves the truth of what Greavsie always says: 'Football really is a funny old game'.

Enjoy!

Mike Bassett

Kick-Off by Ricky Tomlinson

I have always collected football stories like other people collect stamps, and it's great to get this opportunity to stick them into a book.

You can't grow up in Liverpool without being football mad, and whether you're Liverpool red blooded or Everton blue there's always something to make you laugh. While I'm red at heart, I had a foot in both camps as a kid. My mam, God bless her, was a cleaner at Goodison Park and later worked in the canteen at Anfield, serving tea and meat pies. She told me that Bill Shankly was very partial to a biscuit with his cuppa. One day she said to him, 'Would you like a garibaldi, Mr Shankly?'

'None of that foreign rubbish,' he growled in his punctured-bagpipes accent. 'Gi'e me a good Scottish shortbread. Now that's a *sensible* biscuit.'

So I have straddled the red/blue divide on Merseyside (which can make your eyes water, believe me), and when I'm watching football I am much more Jim Royle than Joe Royle. I let the players know just what I think if they're not doing their job properly. If they're playing like a bunch of bananas I say so, and make sure they hear. It goes with the territory, just as I have to accept hecklers if I am stinking up a stage.

Back in the days when I sweated buckets on the building sites earning my daily bread as a plasterer I went to Anfield for my leisure and pleasure, and I expected (and usually got) value for my money. The players under Shanks never used to shirk, and always got as sweaty as I did. We all worked our gollocks off. These days I see players coming off the pitch with their shirts as dry as when they left the dressing-room, and that makes me flaming angry. They have wallets as high as the Himalayas, but in many cases give a thimbleful in effort. That's cheating in my book.

My love of the game goes back more than fifty years. I can remember when footballers played for little more than you pay for a packet of fags today. My schoolboy idol was Billy Liddell, a Scottish winger who was so good that in those days they called Liverpool Liddellpool. In his entire career he earned less than David Beckham picks up in a week. No wonder Posh calls him Golden Balls.

We loved Jocks at Anfield. Liddell, Kenny Dalglish, Ian St John, Graeme Souness, Ron Yeats, Alan Hansen and Tommy 'The Flying Pig' Lawrence, to name just a few. And, of course, when Liverpool were founded after Everton walked out on Anfield back in the days of Victoria – Queen, not Posh – the first Reds team was made up of ten Scots and an English goalkeeper called McOwen.

But now the Macs have given way to the XYZ-men – foreign players with unpronounceable names. They wear the red shirts with a lot of panache, but perhaps not the same passion as in the good old/bad old days when players could kick each other up in the air without the referee running around waving cards like a demented Paul Daniels. Mind you, the miraculous victory over AC Milan in the 2005 European Champions' Cup final made me eat a lot of my words, and I had to hold my hands up and admit that was as good as it gets. Our local lads Steven Gerrard and Jamie Carragher proved that they could look any of the ghosts of Liverpool's great past in the eye, and 'Pole Dancer' Jerzy Dudek matched even Bruce 'Spaghetti Legs' Grobbelaar with his goal-line antics during the penalty shoot-out.

Before I get to the funny stuff I want to take just a few moments to make some serious points about the so-called Beautiful Game.

The people who run football should be ashamed of themselves

for how they've allowed the game to move out of the reach of many working-class people. They are like bloody pickpockets, the way they steal money to fund the lives of players who are overpaid, overpampered and, in the case of some foreign players, unfortunately over here.

It beats me how parents can afford to take their kids to a match. By the time they've bought their seats, munched a pie, purchased a programme and paid for the petrol there can't be much change, if any, out of seventy quid. And a lot of the spectators are cheering on their team in a club shirt that costs three times more than it should.

I've stopped going to Anfield as a sort of one-man campaign against the exorbitant prices. I could afford to go, of course, but I feel more people should stand up and be counted (or, in these days of all-seater stadiums, make a sit-down protest). Fans need to make the point that they are being ripped off. It's a bloody disgrace, and the sooner the clubs play fair with their supporters, the better. Give the game back to the people.

Now that I've got that off my chest, let's move on to what this book is all about – funny football stories.

Many of the tales I'm about to tell are true, some are apocryphal, and in others I've changed the names to protect the guilty (and to save myself from legal fisticuffs).

I will mix in a few jokes with the stories, like the one about the midnight telephone call that Everton chairman Bill Kenwright received from the fire brigade.

'Sorry, Mr Kenwright, but Goodison is on fire,' said the brigade chief.

'Oh no,' said Bill. 'Whatever you do, please try to save the cups.'

'No worries there,' said the fire chief. 'The blaze hasn't reached the canteen yet.'

Welcome to *Football My Arse!*

Ricky Tomlinson

1 ▷ Tales of the Unexpected

Here's a football trivia question for you. Who was the last manager to give a team talk in the old Wembley dressing-room? Arsène Wenger? Sir Alex Ferguson? Sir Bobby Robson? Get ready to bow your knee in respect. It was *me*! I was portraying Mike Bassett, the hapless boss of the England team, in the film of the same name. The bulldozers were parked down Wembley Way ready to start the demolition of the Twin Towers, and the producers coughed up sixty thousand smackers to re-lay the pitch so that we could stage a game for the cameras. It was the last ever match at the old Wembley, the cathedral of football where the ghosts of English football past have hundreds of tales to tell.

I gave my team talk in the same home dressing-room where Sir Alf Ramsey rallied the English troops before the victorious battle in the 1966 World Cup final, and where Shanks had stoked up the Liverpool players to get them in the mood to bring the FA Cup to Anfield for the first time the year before. There I was, giving my Churchillian speech to the England team, reading my notes off the back of a packet of fags and doing my best to sound as inspirational as the likes of Sir Alf, Shanks and Sir Matt Busby all rolled into one. But, being Mike Bassett, it all came out more like a mix of Yosser Hughes, Ken Dodd and a Scouse Alf Garnett.

I had great fun making *Mike Bassett*, which was so successful that we got a transfer to television. The highlight for me, apart

The King and I. Me with the peerless Pele during the shooting of *Mike Bassett* in Brazil. I am telling him that Geoff Hurst's goal in the 1966 World Cup final was at least two feet over the line . . . give or take a foot!

from the Wembley experience, was travelling to Brazil to shoot a scene in the Maracana Stadium – right up there with Wembley as the most famous football ground in the world, and the location of a 1950 World Cup match between Uruguay and Brazil that was watched by a world-record crowd of 200,000.

Pele – the King – agreed to a walk-on part in a key scene shot in the heart of Rio. It was set in a bar while the England World Cup challenge was rapidly turning from football to farce. The team captain had been arrested and my star player was caught out trying to have a bit of how's your father with a statuesque Brazilian beauty who – surprise, surprise – turned out to be a fella. The British tabloid press were giving me – well, Mike Bassett – terrible stick, and I was looking for the answer to my problems in the bottom of a glass. I got rat-arsed in the film and was photographed dancing on the bar wearing just a pair of underpants. Not a pretty sight! At this point, Pele was scripted to walk in, cast his eye over the scene of drunken disorder and then look at me. His one line was, 'Oh no, not the English.' Just as he was about to deliver it, I went arse over tit off the bar. Pele bent double with laughter and could not get his line out. I told him I'd had a stiff one too many, and I wasn't referring to his Viagra TV commercial.

So now I can always claim that I appeared at Wembley and the Maracana, and I (sort of) played alongside Pele.

A true story that Pele told us while waiting for the cameras to roll was that he was going to be dropped from the Brazilian World Cup squad before the 1970 finals – because he was short-sighted! The manager Joao Saldanha, a former journalist, a poet, philosopher and one-time revolutionary, told Pele he was worried about his eyesight and that he felt it would be in the team's interest to leave him out of the squad. *Doh!* It would have been a bit like dropping Lennon *and* McCartney from The Beatles. The story was leaked to the press, and it was Saldanha who was sacked. Pele went on to become the first, and so far the only, player to be a World Cup winner three times. How short-sighted could Saldanha get?

Asked if he was short-sighted, Pele (the scorer of more than one thousand goals) replied: 'A little, but I could see the net. That was all that mattered!'

Here are some more tales of the unexpected about footballers and their lives . . .

I had the pleasure of meeting Bob Paisley, a legend at Anfield whose one-man trophy collection has been beaten only by Sir Alex Ferguson. Bob came across as more like a genial uncle than a hard-bitten football manager, and he told this tale of the unexpected with a surprisingly soft Geordie accent:

Liverpool were playing Huddersfield in a League match in the late 1940s. Those were the days when the referee used to leave the match ball on the centre-spot at half-time because spectators knew their place and would not dare put a foot on the sacred turf.

We came out and lined up for the start of the second half and it was Huddersfield to kick off. I can see it now as clearly as if it were yesterday – the great Peter Doherty, wearing the number-ten shirt for Huddersfield, jogging up and down in anticipation as he waited for his centre-forward to tap the ball to him.

The whistle blew and off we went. Peter was quickly away on one of his magical weaving runs through our defence when suddenly the whistle went again for no apparent reason. We looked up in bewilderment to see the ref and his two linesmen approaching the pitch from the players' tunnel.

The ref was blowing an Eddie Calvert trumpet solo on his whistle to get us to stop the game so that he could get on to the pitch. We had started the game without him thanks to a joker in the crowd who had a whistle with him!

A wonderful tale of the unexpected comes from Kevin Keegan, one of my all-time favourite Liverpool players who many people on Merseyside have still not forgiven for ducking off – like The Beatles – to Hamburg:

England were playing Poland at Wembley in the vital World Cup qualifier in 1973. It was a game we had to win and the Poles were holding us to 1–1, with Tomaszewski – the man famously labelled a clown by Brian Clough – playing an absolute blinder in the Polish goal.

Bobby Moore, who had been dropped, was sitting alongside manager Sir Alf Ramsey on the bench. I was sitting to Bobby's right along with the other substitutes, including my Liverpool team-mate Ray Clemence and Derby forward Kevin Hector.

The game was into the last few minutes and I couldn't understand why Alf hadn't sent on a substitute to try to nick the winner that would have taken us into the World Cup finals. Alf was never comfortable using substitutes because they had not been allowed in his playing days, and had been introduced only after the 1966 World Cup.

Suddenly, with just five minutes to go and under nagging pressure from Bobby Moore, Alf finally decided he should send on a sub. 'Kevin, get stripped,' he ordered.

This was the moment when the drama on the bench turned to farce. Ray Clemence helped me off with my tracksuit bottoms, but he was so eager that he tugged my shorts down to my knees. While I was suffering this overexposure I became even further embarrassed when Alf made it clear he meant Kevin Hector not me!

By the time the other Kevin got on there were just a hundred seconds left – the shortest England debut on record. What's not so funny is that England went out of the World Cup, Alf eventually lost his job and the clown was hailed as a hero at home in Poland. We had been polished off.

Kevin Keegan was back at Wembley a few months later with Liverpool, and got involved in an astonishing punch-up with Leeds skipper Billy Bremner in the Charity Shield match. Kevin lost his temper after two challenges in quick succession from Johnny Giles and Bremner. In reflective mood some years later, Kevin recalled: 'I allowed myself to be provoked by the infamous Leeds tactics, first an off-the-ball whack from Giles followed soon afterwards by a crafty dig from Bremner that brought on the red mist of temper. I went after Bremner and we were both ordered off after swapping wildly aimed punches. Neither Billy nor I could explain why, as we walked off, we both pulled off our shirts in disgust.'

The incident was seen by millions on television at a time when the game was under the microscope because of increasing violence on the pitch and the escalating hooliganism problem.

The establishment was more upset by the disrespectful shirt-stripping than the punches, and they were determined to make an example of both players. They were both punished with what was then a massive five-hundred-pound fine plus a five-week suspension.

Ken Dodd's catchphrase 'Where's me shirt?' was popular at the time, and the answer on Merseyside became, 'Our Kev's just taken it off.'

Remember that wonderful photograph of Vinnie Jones squeezing Paul Gascoigne's bits and pieces? Gazza responded by sending a single rose to Vinnie, who could not let it end there. He arranged a special delivery to Gazza of a loo brush. Maybe that's why England manager Bobby Robson called him 'as daft as a brush'.

Robbie Fowler always seems a bit of a lovable scally to me, with his Toxteth roots clearly visible. I don't think there were many finer strikers in the game when he was really motoring for the Reds. The day he mimed sniffing the touchline as if it were a line of coke after scoring against Everton was an act of madness that earned him a six-match ban. As funny as it was to watch, it's not the sort of thing footballing role models should be showing the kids.

Fowler then went a Stamford Bridge too far when repeatedly flashing his bum to England team-mate Graeme Le Saux during a Liverpool game at Chelsea. The TV cameras caught Le Saux taking his revenge by whacking Fowler on the head from behind. It all led to Le Saux getting some terrible stick from homophobic fans around the country. The England defender found himself reduced to having to deny that he was gay. It gave a whole new unsavoury meaning to football my arse!

Le Saux was involved in an even more amazing incident when playing for Blackburn Rovers in a Champions League match in

Moscow in 1995. He and Rovers team-mate David Batty had a full-scale punch-up on the pitch after they had collided. Skipper Tim Sherwood had to pull the two of them apart. Manager Ray Harford fined each of them two weeks' wages, and said, 'Save your temper for the opposition.'

There's a sort of morbid fascination in watching team-mates fall out, a bit like seeing temperamental actors tearing into each other on set. Not that this ever happens, of course (and if you believe that, you'll believe Rock Hudson was straight). There was a cracker at Anfield in 1993 involving the Reds' eccentric goalkeeper Bruce Grobbelaar and a young Steve McManaman. Steve mishit a clearance that led to Everton scoring against Liverpool. Bruce went potty at Steve, who reacted by shouting back. Instead of leaving it at just verbals at six paces, Grobbelaar then grabbed hold of his team-mate by the throat and seemed ready to strangle him. Somebody in the Kop shouted, 'Don't worry, Steve. He can't hold anything for long.'

Stan Collymore – let's call him a dogged player – had an on-pitch row with his Leicester City side-kick Trevor Benjamin when playing against Charlton that spilled over into the dressing-room. They both put their fists where their mouths were, and Stan the Man refused to go out for the second half. He was soon shown the door by Leicester, where he had previously got himself in deep water by letting off a fire extinguisher in a hotel bar in La Manga.

Stan blew hot and cold when he joined Liverpool; a sort of Collymore-or-less. He had the ability to be one of the all-time great finishers, but seemed to me to be in a weird world of his own. Liverpool have always based their play on teamwork, but in my opinion he was too much of a self-centred individualist. On Merseyside now he is known as 'Stan who?' When he was caught by a tabloid paper 'dogging' – watching couples at it in deserted car parks – a Kopite said, 'I always knew he'd go to the dogs.'

Two clashes share top billing in this collection of team-mate fights. First was the extraordinary punch-up between Charlton's Derek Hales and Mike Flanagan in an FA Cup third-round tie against Maidstone at the Valley. There were five minutes to go and the score stood at 1–1 when Flanagan played a through-ball to Hales that caught him offside.

'Why the blankety-blank didn't you give the pass earlier?' shouted Hales.

They ran at each other and started exchanging punches in a free-for-all that finished with them both being sent to the dressing-room. Even Flanagan and Allen could not have matched it for comedy.

Then, of course, there were the fisticuffs between Newcastle team-mates Lee Bowyer and Kieran Dyer that got them both red-carded against Aston Villa at St James' Park in April 2005. When it was reported that Dyer had been fined £200,000, boxing promoter Frank Warren apparently said: 'For that, I would want Mike Tyson . . . not handbags at six paces.'

How good was Duncan Edwards, the Busby Babe who perished in the Munich air disaster that wiped out half the Manchester United team in 1958? No less a person than Sir Bobby Charlton, British football's greatest ambassador, provides this memory of Duncan that captures his standing in the game:

> *Duncan was the complete player. Good with both feet, strong in the tackle, commanding in the air, a powerful shot and an accurate passer of the ball no matter what the distance. He could play in any position and had the ability to dictate and dominate any match.*
>
> *I remember one particular game when I was playing with Duncan for the Army against the RAF during our National Service. Duncan received the ball from our goalkeeper deep in*

our half, passed it to the full-back and took the return pass. Then he exchanged passes with me, stroked the ball to another forward, quickly demanded it back and unleashed the hardest shot you're ever likely to see from the edge of the box. The ball rocketed towards the goalkeeper's head. He ducked out of the way and the ball crashed into the net.

Quite a few years later I was walking down a street in Cambridge when a chap stopped me. 'You don't remember me, do you, Bobby?' he said. 'I played against you some time back when you were in the Army team.'

The game came back to me, and I asked him which position he played.

'Goalie,' he said.

When I reminded him how he had ducked out of the way of Duncan's shot, he replied, 'Yes, that was the proudest moment of my life.'

There are scores of stories (the operative word) about the late, great George Best, most of them true. My favourite is the old classic that George told at the drop of a drink. It's the often repeated one about the time when he was, um, looking after one of the three Miss Worlds who were among his string of conquests. He took her to a casino where he won twenty grand with one spin of the wheel. George cashed in his chips, and, with the money stashed into his pockets and Miss World on his arm, ordered a chauffeured limousine back to the Manchester hotel where they were staying.

As the wizened little Irish night porter let them in, George tipped him twenty quid to bring a bottle of chilled Dom Perignon up to their room.

Miss World, in a see-through negligée, was just coming out of the bathroom and the twenty grand was spread over the bed when the porter arrived with the champagne. As he put the tray on the bedside table, he asked a little nervously, 'I wonder, George, if you mind a fellow Ulsterman putting a personal question to you?'

'Fire away,' said George, peeling off another tenner from the stack of money and handing it to his countryman.

'Well, I was wondering,' said the porter, 'where did it all go wrong?'

Bestie once had a heated argument with his good friend David Sadler, the gifted utility player, who accused him of hogging the ball and never giving passes to his team-mates. Every time George got the ball in United's next League match he immediately passed it to the feet of Sadler, who just happened to be playing in the centre of the defence at the time.

In another game – to win a bet with himself – George played the ball throughout the match with his left foot.

He was so idolised in Manchester that when he took a beautiful companion into a local Italian restaurant one evening, the football-daft waiter pulled back George's chair for him to sit down and completely ignored the girl.

And it was George who famously said, with a straight face, 'I spent most of my money on birds, booze and fast cars. I squandered the rest.'

While gathering stories for this book, I found the name of Nobby Stiles popping up a lot. Norbert, to give him his proper moniker, was known around the world as the 'Toothless Tiger' because he always used to leave his false teeth but never, so to speak, his tackle in the dressing-room. He was not the prettiest of sights without his teeth; a Liverpool fan once began a letter to him 'Dear Ugly . . .'

Nobby was labelled a dirty player but he did not maliciously set out to damage anybody. It just happened that he was playing in an era when physical contact was not considered the deadliest sin on the football field. But he was, to say the least, very competitive; the sort of bloke you wanted on your team, not against you. He earned his reputation early in his career for being a tough tackler, but it was more down to bad eyesight than premeditated

Nobby Stiles on duty at his post. He would have kicked his granny to stop Man United or England conceding a goal.

violence. Man United manager Sir Matt Busby once caught him squinting at the team-sheet so he sent him to the optician, who advised contact lenses. He then developed into one of the world's great midfield anchormen, a ball-winner out of the old school. But off the pitch Nobby remained a walking disaster area.

Like me, he was as blind as the proverbial bat without his glasses. He once went 'missing' from an England after-match banquet in a swish hotel in Gothenburg. He had left the dinner-table to go to the gents', but after he had been gone for an hour his team-mates were starting to wonder whether they should send out a search party. Just then a red-faced Nobby reappeared, laughing as he explained where he had been. 'I left my glasses here at the table,' he said. 'When I came out of the loo I managed to walk into the banqueting suite next door. I was wandering around looking for our table, and it was ages before I realised I was at somebody's wedding reception.'

Once, when he was driving through Manchester, his car ran into the one in front at some traffic lights. He and the other driver jumped out to inspect the damage, and as they bent down they cracked their heads together.

On another occasion Nobby gave relatives a lift to Manchester Piccadilly Station. After he had seen them off he discovered he had mislaid his car keys. He went through every pocket several times, then retraced his steps to the platform barrier where he had waved goodbye. Still no sign of his keys. Finally he called a taxi, returned home to pick up his spare set and then had the cabbie drive him back to his car. He paid the fare for the two-way journey, sat behind the wheel of his car and found his missing keys. They were still in the ignition.

Nobby and his team-mate Paddy Crerand went to a Roman Catholic mass together in Madrid on the eve of Manchester United's 1968 European Cup semi-final against Real Madrid. When Nobby put a pile of pesetas in the collection box Paddy whispered, 'No good trying to bribe Him, Nobby. We've got to win this one ourselves.'

The next day the United players were given a hostile farewell as they left the Bernabeu Stadium after a memorable victory. Nobby – it had to be accident-waiting-to-happen Nobby – got clonked on the head by a bottle. Paddy Crerand waved at the supporters as they spat and screamed at the team coach. But while smiling in an apparently friendly fashion, he was shouting, 'Muchos bollockos . . .'

Paddy told this true Irish story about a Manchester United close-season trip to Dublin:

I was with a few of the lads who fancied a drink and we decided to go outside Dublin and find a nice country pub. We gave instructions to a cab driver and he took us about ten miles outside of town to a pleasant little place where the main trade came from summer holidaymakers.

We found a pub in the high street, but it had the 'Closed' sign up.

The publican noticed us and came out all apologetic. 'Sorry, we won't be open for another half-hour,' he said. 'Would you be liking a drink while you're waiting?'

Later I was at the bar getting a round in when I asked the barmaid, 'When d'you close, love?'

She replied, 'The end of September.'

Here's one more story about the wonderful Man United all-stars team of the 1960s. This one's about Denis 'the Menace' Law, one of the greatest strikers I've ever clapped eyes on. He had such quick reflexes in the penalty area that they called him the Electric Heel. He always marked his goals with a flamboyant punch in the air.

Injury forced him out of the crucial 1968 European Cup semifinal against Real Madrid, and he sat alongside manager Matt Busby on the bench. He was so excited by a Bill Foulkes goal that he punched the air in his inimitable style. His fist smashed against the roof of the dugout and he broke a bone in his hand. Denis had been dogged by a depressing run of injuries at the time, and as his damaged hand was being treated he said, 'Marvellous! I even get injured *watching* the game.'

At the start of the noble campaign to stamp racism out of football in the 2004–05 season a journalist covering the Millwall–Brighton game at the New Den sent a report back to the office saying that spectators were chanting 'Sieg Heil' at the players. The tabloid sports editor was ready to give the fans some heavy stick in an article when it was pointed out that the reporter had actually heard the Brighton fans shouting the club nickname: 'Seagulls . . . Seagulls.'

If that cloth-eared reporter had covered the Nuremberg rallies, it might have been documented that Hitler was being warned by thousands of his followers that some birds were overhead and that he was in danger of being shat on.

Wouldn't it be great if players, managers and referees were totally honest with their after-match comments? They should use German goalkeeper Harald Schumacher (try keeping up with him!) as their role model.

After a shocker of a match in the Bundesliga he was asked for his comments by a reporter. He did not duck behind the usual 'the sun was in my eyes . . . the ball was muddy' excuses. Schumacher said, 'I played like an arsehole.'

Mind you, I can remember when he was called much worse than that. He committed one of the most brutal fouls ever seen in a World Cup match. France and West Germany were drawing 1–1 in the 1982 semi-final when Schumacher nearly killed French substitute Patrick Battiston. He came rushing off his line and chopped down the striker with what could only be described as a high-flying assault rather than a tackle.

I was one of the millions staring at the television in total disbelief when the referee not only allowed Schumacher to stay on the pitch but did not even rule it as a foul.

Poor Battiston was carried off unconscious with an oxygen mask on his face, and minus three teeth. French skipper Michel Platini later reported that he was convinced Battiston was dead because he could not find a pulse.

In a poll conducted by a French newspaper the next day, Schumacher was voted the most unpopular man in France. Adolf Hitler came second.

Nils Liedholm is not a well-known name in the UK, but on the Continent the Swede is revered as one of the all-time great midfield marshals and is considered the finest passer of a ball that ever breathed. One incident that illustrates just how precise he was came during a game he was playing for Milan in the 1950s. He mishit a pass that went to the feet of an opponent. There was a collective sharp intake of breath, and somebody shouted, 'It's a miracle. Liedholm has misplaced a pass.' In three years with Milan, nobody could remember such a thing. A ripple of applause around the San Siro Stadium grew into a roar, and for five minutes the entire crowd cheered Liedholm, just so he knew how much his accuracy had been treasured and appreciated.

We used to give similar applause on the Kop to Tommy Smith if ever he *found* a team-mate with a pass. If you're reading this, Tommy, I'm only joking. If you're not reading it, you couldn't pass for toffee.

Tommy Smith remains a bruise on the memory of a procession of forwards. He used to make *me* jump, and I was just standing on the Kop!

In one match at Anfield he was having a verbal exchange with Coventry's Scottish international dribbler Tommy Hutchison.

Hutch decided on a novel way to settle their argument. 'Tell you what, Smithy,' he said, 'I'll race you to the halfway line for your wages.'

The Anfield iron man knew that strength rather than speed was his ace. 'You're on,' he said, 'but only if we then have a double-or-nothing wager on a scrap afterwards.'

Hutch politely declined the offer. Wise man.

There would be a lot of competition as to who has been the wackiest foreign footballer to take the English pound. Eric Cantona made himself a candidate for the title with his infamous karate kick against a Crystal Palace supporter who had bad-mouthed him.

Legal eagles got involved, and hard-bitten football reporters, reared on 'over the moon, Brian' and 'sick as a parrot' quotes, looked on dumbstruck when the Frenchman told them after a judge had quashed a jail sentence: 'When seagulls follow a trawler it is because they think sardines will be thrown into the sea.'

That was the extent of his reaction at the news conference. The press boys were, well, as sick as parrots. It made me think that Red Eric was a claw short of a full lobster.

But Cantona is as sane as the Seine compared to a Dutchman who rejoices in the name of Marco Boogers. West Ham signed him for a million pounds in 1995, and – coming on as a substitute – he hardly got a sniff of action before he was red-carded for a vicious tackle on Man United's Gary Neville. In total he made four substitute appearances (that's £250,000 a go) before disappearing not only from West Ham but from the country. It was weeks before he was found hiding in a caravan in deepest Holland. He sent a sick note saying he had suffered some sort of nervous breakdown.

'I bought him on the evidence of a video sequence of his best moments,' said Hammers manager Harry Redknapp. 'He was a good player but a nutter. They didn't show that on the video.'

Branco, a Brazilian who was an expensive flop at Middlesbrough, amazed his team-mates before one League match when he stood up in the dressing-room and delivered the following tactical talk as he mimed kicking the ball: 'Pass . . . pass . . . pass . . . Goal! . . . Lager . . . lager . . . Nightclub!'

What a ball so many of these foreign players are having as they stuff their pockets with supporters' hard-earned cash. Take Ilie Dumitrescu, for instance. The Romanian, who was outstanding in the 1994 World Cup finals, featured on a double-page picture spread of a Sunday tabloid within three weeks of bringing his ball skills to Tottenham. A photographer snatched pictures of him having his way on the back seat of his car with a young lady who turned out to be a London policewoman. You're nicked. Or should that be knickers?

Another Romanian, Florin Raducioiu, managed to reduce Harry Redknapp to speechless fury when he failed to show up for the team coach taking the West Ham players to a midweek evening match. Harry called him on his mobile and said, 'Where the blankety-blank are you? The coach is about to leave.'

'Leave for what?' said Florin.

'For the match, you pillock,' shouted Harry.

'We're playing today?' said our hero. 'Oh, I forget. I am out shopping.'

'Shopping?' screamed Harry. 'You're shopping! Where are you shopping?'

'Harvey Nichols,' said Florin. Absolutely fabulous!

With that, Harry threw down his mobile and ordered the coach driver to leave a player short.

From then on, Harry considered Raducioiu shop soiled.

When he was manager of Newcastle United, Ruud Gullit shelled out £5.8 million for Spanish international defender Elena Marcelino. Four years and just fourteen games later he was on his way back to Spain. 'The fans called me a thieving gypsy who was robbing their club,' he said following his escape.

Newcastle chairman Freddy Shepherd summed it all up when he commented, 'They say you should only say good things about people. With this in mind I'll just say he's gone. Good!'

The funniest foreign transfer deal saw Graeme Souness and Southampton being sucked into a scam that was hilarious for everybody looking on from the outside. Souness received a call from someone claiming to be George Weah, World Player of the Year, recommending that he sign his cousin from Senegal, one Ali Dia. The manager fell for it hook, line and, as it turned out, stinker.

Dia was signed and appeared as a substitute against Leeds. Souness watched with open mouth as Dia struggled to control the ball and ran around like a headless chicken with no idea of positioning. The dire Dia was summoned off after fifty-three minutes, and never kicked another ball for Southampton. He joined non-League Gateshead and was equally useless with them. George Weah later said, 'Ali Dia? Never heard of him.' Ali Dia? More like Ali oops!

After Southampton won the FA Cup in 1976 – shocking Man United at Wembley – they somehow managed to put the treasured trophy in the keeping of the old King of the King's Road, Peter Osgood. He had plenty of partying experience at Chelsea to call on, and was leading the celebrations when suddenly entrusted with the job of making sure the FA Cup got back safely to the south coast. It was like putting the *Titanic* entertainments officer in charge of the *Queen Mary*.

At three o'clock in the morning after the final, a seriously sozzled Ossie was showing off the trophy to astonished Saints supporters who were having a coffee at a mobile snack-bar on the A3. Then, as you do, Ossie took the cup home and slept with it! 'It was the best way of looking after it and keeping it safe,' he later explained, using the sort of logic that made sense only to him.

Sadly, they just don't have wonderful characters like Ossie in the game any more.

We should pause here and remember the contribution to the development of football of a certain Mrs Lindon. Her husband, H.J. Lindon, made a living manufacturing footballs, and his wife assisted him. She died from a lung disease caused by blowing up hundreds of pig bladders. This tragedy inspired H.J. to find an alternative to pig bladders, and he developed the first inflatable rubber bladder in 1862. Mrs Lindon has gone down in history for her blow job.

I love this tale of the unexpected about Arsenal's ten-million-pound Spanish forward José Reyes. He admitted practising his dribbling against a mass defence of a dozen gnomes in the garden of his North London mansion. 'It helps sharpen my reflexes,' said José. I heard it whispered that he was beaten once. It's known in football as a gnome defeat.

Reyes was on the receiving end of one of the most bizarre goal celebrations ever after he had scored for Seville in a La Liga match against Valladolid. His team-mate Francisco Gallardo pulled him to the ground, reached down into his shorts and started to, um, make a meal of his penis! The entire incident was captured in close-up by television cameras, and the Spanish authorities charged Gallardo with misconduct. Reyes was not amused when his team-mate dismissed it as 'a lot of fuss over such a small thing'.

'Jinky' Jimmy Johnstone was a winger with Jock Stein's Celtic and could best be described as like Stanley Matthews on speed. He used to make as many headlines off the pitch as on it with his wayward, often drink-fuelled, behaviour.

Once, when preparing for a Home Championship match against England at Hampden Park, he and some high-spirited team-mates took a break from the coastal training camp for a night on the town. On the way back to the hotel Jinky jumped into a rowing boat and one of the other players gave it a push with his foot. It floated off into the darkness with the wee man – a non-swimmer – standing up singing 'Scotland the Brave'. Suddenly Jimmy realised that the boat had no oars and it was leaking. Then it got caught in a current and was heading to the open sea when the coastguard came to his rescue. Jimmy got a big bollocking from the Scottish FA, but they were not silly enough to drop him. He played a blinder on the Saturday to help Scotland sink England 2–0.

London-born defender Terry Mancini was making his international debut for the Republic of Ireland, who had picked him after discovering that his granny had once sniffed a shillelagh. As he lined up with his new team-mates in the pre-match rituals, he grew restless during what seemed to him an interminably long rendering of the Polish national anthem. Standing to attention, he whispered to team-mate Don Givens, 'This is going on for bloody ever. What's ours like?'

'You're listening to it,' said Givens.

Trevor 'Tosh' Chamberlain was a legend in his own half-time at Fulham, and a procession of stories about this popular Cockney character have gone down in football folklore. Three will give you a glimpse of why he is so warmly remembered at Craven Cottage, where he remains a cult figure.

England skipper Johnny Haynes, whom Fulham made the first hundred-pound-a-week footballer, was good mates with Tosh. But he used to nag the life out of him on the pitch because – like most players – Tosh could not meet Johnny's perfectionist standards. In one First Division match a pass from Haynes was too far ahead of Tosh for him to reach it. Before the King of Craven Cottage could blame him, Tosh turned and shouted, 'You c***!'

Mervyn Griffiths, a top-rate referee from Wales, stopped the game and booked Chamberlain. 'But, Ref,' protested Tosh, 'I can call him a c*** if I want to. He's on *my* side.'

There were times when Tosh could really turn it on and look as devastating as any winger in the League. He hit a purple patch in one particular game and kept going past his rival full-back as if he wasn't there. He skinned him for the umpteenth time and then went on to score a spectacular goal. As he was making his way back to the halfway line, Tosh heard the full-back mutter to a team-mate, 'If that flash bastard goes past me once more I'll break his f***ing leg!'

In this match Fulham were giving a young debutant winger his big chance. Instead of lining up in his usual outside-left position for the kick-off, Tosh crossed to the right wing and told the new lad, 'OK, son, I've ruined that full-back. Now you go over there and have a go. I'll fill in for you here.'

Playing at Orient, Fulham won a corner out on the left. Tosh was so busy looking to see where to place the ball that when he took the kick he missed completely and kicked the corner-flag out of the ground. It gave a whole new meaning to being disoriented.

Back in the days before players had their names on their shirts, witty Tottenham and Northern Ireland skipper Danny Blanchflower was introducing the Duchess of Kent to the Spurs players before the 1961 FA Cup final against Leicester City.

'Tell me,' said the Duchess, 'why is it that the other team have their names on the backs of their tracksuits while your team do not?'

'Well, you see, ma'am,' said Danny, 'we all *know* each other.'

When he was on Sunderland's books, striker Kevin Phillips was stopped for speeding. He was told it would mean three points on his licence. 'No chance, I suppose, of you giving the points to the team?' asked Phillips.

Here's a story that has been circulating for years, but few people give the right player the credit for the classic gag. It was Birmingham City defender Gary Pendrey who got booked for a rugged tackle in a League match in the 1970s.

'Do that again and you're off,' warned the referee.

'But what was the matter with the tackle, Ref?' asked Pendrey, spreading his arms in a gesture of innocence.

'It was a late tackle,' snapped the referee.

'But I got there as fast as I could,' said Pendrey.

I will finish this tales of the unexpected collection the way I started, with a Bob Paisley story. He was a real joker on the quiet, always looking to wind people up and then make it look as if others were the culprits. It was never done with malice, but just good-fun leg-pulls. One story he always told came from the days when he was the assistant to Don Welsh, Liverpool manager before the arrival of Bill Shankly.

Welsh used to get his car washed every week by a Liverpool docker called Paddy Walsh, a giant Irishman who was potty about the Reds and always at the club offering to do odd jobs. He used to throw buckets of water over the manager's car and then dry and polish. Bob watched him one week as he filled his bucket. Just as he was about to start throwing the water, an apprentice, primed by Bob, told Paddy the boss wanted him. Paddy wandered off, couldn't find the manager anywhere and so returned to his car-washing job. While he was away Bob had wound down the driver's window. Paddy didn't notice and looked on in horror as the bucket of water he threw at the car went straight in and soaked the two front seats. Apparently Paddy said, 'Bucket,' or something similar.

Bob Paisley took his football seriously, but he always found time for a laugh. That's the way it should be. I wish some of the miserable gits running the game today could learn from his approach.

You've gotta laugh

Sven-Goran Eriksson walks into the England dressing-room after a defeat, shaking his head in despair. 'The Football Association committee is putting pressure on me to drop you because you're all stupid,' he says to the players. 'What I have decided to do is ask a simple question of one of you, and if he gets it right, you will all be in my next squad. Now, please choose somebody to represent you.'

The players nominate skipper David Beckham to answer the question because they consider him the most intelligent among them.

Eriksson looks at him intently through his rimless glasses and says, 'OK, David, please concentrate hard. What is five plus six?'

Becks thinks for a moment, a frown on his forehead as he does the mental arithmetic, and then, a little hesitantly, he answers, 'Eleven?'

'Eleven!' Eriksson shouts loudly, excited that his captain got it right.

The other players, mistaking Eriksson's excitement for disappointment, plead in unison, 'Come on, Boss, give him another chance!'

Hark who's talking

Sir Bobby Robson:
'That little lad Paul Parker has jumped like a salmon and tackled like a ferret.'

Ian Wright:
'It took a lot of bottle for Tony Adams to own up to being an alcoholic.'

Kenny Sansom:
'His testimonial will be such an emotional night for Tony Adams. I can't wait to go for a drink with him afterwards.'

Graham Roberts:
'Football's a game of skill . . . We kicked them, and they kicked us back.'

Ugo Ehiogu:
'I'm as happy as I can be – but I have been happier.'

Tommy Docherty:
'We put bells in the ball so Jim Holton would know where it was. We had complaints from morris dancers saying he was kicking them all over the place.'

Mick Lyons:
'If there wasn't such a thing as football, we'd all be frustrated footballers.'

Sammy Nelson:
'They can crumble as easily as ice-cream in this heat.'

Sir Matt Busby:
'Nobby Stiles a dirty player? No, he's never deliberately hurt anybody. Mind you, he's frightened quite a few!'

Ron Greenwood:
'Bobby Moore was sent on this earth with ice in his veins.'

Sir Alf Ramsey:
'Bobby Moore could play in his overcoat and not break into a sweat.'

John Carey:
'Trying to tackle Stanley Matthews is like trying to tackle a ghost.'

Stuart Pearce:
'I can see the carrot at the end of the tunnel.'

Ashley Cole:
'I don't think players care too much about stats and statistics.'

Sergei Baltacha:
'In Russia we play the ball first. Since defending in Britain I have discovered that there are times when it is the man who is played first. But I am learning.'

Ray Wilson:
'After I had become a funeral director, Greavsie said no wonder I was so good in the box. I told him to stand still while I measured him. That shut the lovely little sod up.'

Stuart Pearce:
'When I cocked up the penalty in the 1990 World Cup shoot-out I wanted to hide in a hole. I think it was Gazza who said I would have missed the hole!'

David Webb:
'The referee said, "What's your name?" I said, "Number six."'

George Cohen:
'Alf Ramsey had a stare that could melt ice from ten feet.'

Joe Mercer:
'The hardest tackler I ever saw or played with was Wilf Copping. He had a tackle that made Norman Hunter seem about as ferocious as Andy Pandy.'

Vic Buckingham:
'Wilf Copping didn't bite your legs. He bit your bollocks.'

Brian Clough:
'Until we got hold of him, Kenny Burns couldn't crush a grape with a tackle. Now Big Daddy would be frightened of going near him.'

Alfred (Lord) Kinnaird:
'I came home with a broken leg, and Mother wanted to know to whom it belonged.'

Malcolm Allison:
'Size does matter in football. You judge a defender by the size of his tackle.'

Frank McLintock:
'Seeing the ball go into our net was as painful as having your testicles squeezed in nutcrackers.'

Jack Charlton:
'If it's a toss up between making a winning tackle or landing a big fish, I think for me the fish wins.'

Ron 'Chopper' Harris:
'I was once asked if I kick opponents deliberately. I replied, "Only if they get in my way deliberately."'

Graeme Le Saux:
'The opening ceremony was good, although I missed it.'

2 Getting Netted

Football without goals would be like sex without the orgasm. It was no less an authority than former England manager Terry Venables who came up with this parallel theory between scoring on the pitch and in bed. 'Just listen to the crowd during a goal-scoring move,' he said. 'It starts with the low moaning of expectancy in the early stages of a sort of foreplay, and then builds and builds as the ball gets closer to the goal. Then come the screams of ecstasy as it finds the net. *Whoosh!*' Bloody hell, El Tel makes it sound like the second coming.

Yes, goals are the lifeblood of the game, and this chapter concentrates on the funniest, the daftest and most outrageous goals that have helped put a smile on the face of football.

It's my belief that the best liars make the best goalscorers. Goalscoring geniuses like Thierry Henry, Ruud van Nistelrooy and golden oldies such as Roger Hunt, Denis Law and Jimmy Greaves have always been able to convince defenders they are going to do one thing when all the time they know they are going to do something else. They lie with their feet, their swivelling hips and their dipping shoulders, sending defenders one way while they set off in a different direction. The finest players are like those market-place shysters who con punters with 'find the lady' trickery. Now you see the ball, now you don't. A wizard like Ryan Giggs, George Best or Stanley Matthews, for instance, could sell a dummy so well that defenders would almost have to pay to get back in the ground after being sent the wrong way.

The best description I've ever read of a dummy being sold was written by Geoffrey Green, the *Times* correspondent who was acknowledged as one of the all-time great football reporters. He was in the press box that famous day in November 1953 when Hungary thrashed England 6–3, the first ever victory by a foreign team at Wembley. This is how Green described one of the goals by the fabulous Ferenc Puskas, who was being marked by England skipper Billy Wright: 'Puskas pulled the ball back with the sole of his left foot as if loading a rifle and all in the same movement shot it low and true into the far corner of the net. Billy Wright was left tackling thin air like a fire engine going in the wrong direction for the blaze.' Puskas had lied with that magical left foot of his and convinced one of England's greatest defenders that he was going to dribble rather than shoot. But even the Galloping Major – the rank he held in the Hungarian army without ever seeing a parade ground – could not deceive quite like Diego Maradona, the little general from Argentina.

Just think of one of the greatest goals ever scored – Maradona's second against England in the 1986 World Cup quarter-final in Mexico. He glided his way past six England defenders with clever changes of pace and dazzling ball control before applying the deadly accurate finish, rolling the ball into the net after convincing goalkeeper Peter Shilton that he was going to smash it. Maradona must have told half a dozen lies on the way to that goal in a million, but the little toe-rag had told his biggest lie four minutes earlier when he punched the ball into the net for his 'Hand of God' goal. Next to Pele, Maradona was probably the finest footballer ever to step on to a pitch. He could have made himself a role model to kids across the world if he had owned up to using his hand when the unsighted referee awarded a goal. But instead he chose to celebrate his cheating moment by strutting around the pitch as if he owned it. In the space of just four minutes he was responsible for the most stinking and then the most stonking goal scored in the history of the World Cup.

Speaking as a red-blooded Scouser, one of the funniest goals I've seen in recent years was a John Barnes gem in a Premiership game when Liverpool played Southampton at their old Dell ground. Dave Beasant was in goal for the Saints, and in a moment of madness he decided to challenge for a ball out by the left corner flag. He got possession and pirouetted as he cleared the ball with a loose punt upfield. Horror of horrors for Beasant as he saw the ball sail straight to the feet of John Barnes, who was minding his own business in no man's land nearly forty-five yards from the Southampton goal. He drilled an instant shot towards the empty net. Beasant, six foot four of panic-propelled goalie, came charging back into his goal area like a demented daddy-long-legs, and arrived just as the ball was reaching its target. He took a wild lunge, missed and kicked a post as the ball rolled into the net. It was one of those crazy goals you don't cheer because you are too busy choking with laughter. Not that Beasant could see the funny side.

I hope that has put you in the mood for the following goals that all deserve a place in football's chamber of horrors.

Tomas Brolin, a tubby little Swede, had a nightmare after joining Leeds for the small matter of £1.2 million, and in return he played just nineteen games. He had looked streamlined and stunningly skilled when impressing for his country at the 1994 World Cup finals, but had become a bit of a Mr Blobby by the time he arrived at Elland Road a year later. The first of the four goals he scored for the club is remembered with jaw-dropping awe by the Leeds faithful. He miscontrolled a high cross in the Sheffield Wednesday penalty area and managed to fall over the ball. As he lay flat out on the ground a defender's clearance hit him in the stomach. The ball bounced back towards the Wednesday net and the goalkeeper swung at it with his right foot. This time the ball whacked the still-prostrate Brolin on the head and rebounded into the net for a freak goal. Football my farce!

I love the silly goals like the one Marcus Browning scored for Bristol Rovers against Brentford in a League match in 1996. Brentford goalkeeper Kevin Dearden had the ball safely in his hands as Browning challenged him. The danger seemed to be over when Dearden thought he heard the referee's whistle, but the whistle had actually been blown by a spectator. The goalie, thinking he'd been awarded a free-kick, put the ball down at the feet of Browning, who gratefully steered it into the empty net. Goal! Great stuff.

Not far behind in the silly stakes was the goal Gary Crosby scored for Nottingham Forest against Manchester City in 1990. Goalkeeper Andy Dibble caught the ball, and while his defenders ran forward, waiting for his clearance, he balanced the ball on the palm of his hand, looking like a waiter with a tray of drinks. Dibble didn't know that Crosby had run off the pitch behind him and was now returning. He saw the ball being offered on a plate, so to speak, headed it out of the goalkeeper's hand and bundled it into the net, with the distraught Dibble shouting in

'You want the ball? Here, have it!' Young George Best taunts Terry Venables during a Chelsea–Man United match at Old Trafford in 1966. Wonder whatever happened to the pair of 'em?

Copyright ©
popperfoto.com

a mixture of frustration and sheer embarrassment. That's another fine mess you've got yourself in, Officer Dibble!

City manager Howard Kendall could not believe what he was witnessing.

'I haven't got eyes in the back of my head,' groaned Crosby.

'No,' said Howard, 'but you have got two feet. Kick the f***ing thing!'

✦

You would have thought Andy Dibble's experience might have served as a warning to all goalkeepers to take the panto audience advice: 'Behind you.' But Newcastle goalie Shay Given forgot to check in his rear-view mirror during a Premiership match against Coventry in 1997. He caught a high cross, calmly put the ball down on the ground and stepped back to take a run-up. He was one of the few people in the ground who did not know that Dion Dublin was running back on to the pitch behind him. The striker nipped in and stroked the ball into the net, thank you very much. Given had given it away.

✦

Amazingly, the ball burst during the FA Cup finals of 1946 and 1947. Sam Bartram, a larger-than-life character who was the greatest of the uncapped goalkeepers, played in both finals for Charlton. Sam, who later became a respected football reporter with the *Sunday People* after trying his hand at management at Luton, said of the burst-ball incident in the 1946 final against Derby County:

The score was 1–1 when Jackie Stamps, who had the kick of a mule, took a shot that I had covered. As it left his foot there was a hissing sound that we could hear despite the roar of the crowd. When the ball reached me it was a triangular shape and it was all I could do to catch it. I later asked the ref if it would have counted as a goal if the ball had gone into the net, and he said it would have because he could only change it once it was dead. 'Dead?' I said. 'The ball was mortally wounded!' The

odds of it bursting were calculated at a million to one. The fact
that it happened again the following year was beyond belief.

Blow me, if it didn't happen again in a Belgian League match between Anderlecht and La Louviere during the 2004–05 season. The referee allowed a goal when the ball burst on its way into the net from the boot of Anderlecht midfielder Walter Baseggio. But later the Belgian FA decided that the goal should have been disallowed and the game – won 2–1 by Anderlecht – had to be replayed. In their judgement the ball did not meet with FIFA size specifications when it crossed the line. So you see, size *does* matter.

A candidate for the most celebrated goal in history has to be the one headed into the net in injury-time by Japanese forward Naohiro Takahara for Hamburg against Bayern Munich in February 2003. It was Takahara's first goal for the club and he ordered drinks all round: five hundred pints for the supporters crowded into the club bar and another two hundred for team-mates and club officials. It did not cost him a single Euro because a local brewery picked up the tab. Cheers.

And now for something completely different . . . Fasten your safety-belts for an action replay of one of the most extraordinary games in the history of the Beautiful Game. This is not about just one goal, but loads of them.

The venue: the Valley. The date: 21 December 1957. The teams: Charlton Athletic at home to Huddersfield Town, managed by Bill Shankly, two years before he started to build his legend at Liverpool.

Charlton were reduced to ten men early in the first half when their skipper and England international centre-half Derek Ufton was carried off with a broken collarbone. Huddersfield were 0–2 in the lead at half-time, and cantering. Within seven minutes of the second half they had rocketed 1–5 ahead, with the single Charlton goal coming from the right boot of veteran left-winger Johnny Summers.

Huddersfield started to stroll around with the confident air of a team that, understandably, considered they had the game won. After all, they were easily dismantling a defence missing its best player that had conceded 120 goals when being relegated from the First Division the previous season. With just thirty minutes to go, it would need the comeback of the century for Charlton to save the game.

Now for the Summers day. He scored a second goal with a right-foot shot, and a minute later set up team-mate John Ryan for another goal. Charlton 3, Huddersfield 5. Then, over the next ten minutes, Summers added three more goals – all with his right foot – to take his tally to five, and the score to Charlton 6, Huddersfield 5.

Incredible? You ain't seen nothin' yet.

In the eighty-eighth minute, shell-shocked Huddersfield gathered themselves for one more charge and snatched an equaliser. The Valley crowd was dizzy with the excitement of it all, many of them no longer sure what the score was. If Mike Bassett had been managing one of these teams he would have been in an intensive-care unit by now. But there was more to come. Johnny Summers had another trick left up his sleeve. He dashed down the left wing and sent a last-minute pass into the path of Ryan, who hammered it into the net. Charlton 7, Huddersfield 6. No pressman had the courage to tell Shanks that this was the first time in Football League history that a team had scored six goals and lost. For once in his life, Shankly was speechless.

Summers, a chirpy Cockney who had travelled the football roundabout with Fulham, Norwich and Millwall, said, 'I wore these boots for the first time today, and I have never scored a goal with my right foot before. Today I got all five with my right. Amazing, ain't it?'

At the age of just thirty-four, lovely Johnny Summers was cut down by cancer. Suddenly it was winter. But those lucky to have been at the Valley on that astonishing afternoon in December 1957 will always be warmed by the memory of a Summers day.

There was another goal-gorged game in London the following season. Tottenham beat Everton 10–4 in Bill Nicholson's first match in charge as manager at White Hart Lane on 11 October 1958. Tiny schemer Tommy 'the Charmer' Harmer said after a match in which he laid on six goals, 'Don't expect us to do this every week, Boss.'

White Hart Lane was also the venue for what Jimmy Greaves describes as the funniest goal of his career. I will let the goalkeeper on the receiving end tell the tale. Over to the one and only Gordon Banks:

It was one of the craziest goals ever allowed. We [Leicester City] were playing Spurs when they were the best team around. This was in the sixties. The referee awarded Spurs a penalty that we disputed. I remember that it had been raining buckets and there was mud everywhere. There was hardly any grass around in the goal area and I had gone to the back of the net to wipe all the muck off my hands ready to face Greavsie's penalty. The cheeky sod saw I was not in position and side-footed the ball into the other side of the net while I was bending down in the opposite corner. He only did it for a laugh, and was as amazed as everybody else when the twit of a referee signalled a goal. What made it worse was that, instead of telling the ref he was wrong, even my own team-mates were falling about laughing. Happy days.

Now you understand when I say the humour has gone out of the game. Imagine that happening today? There would be a riot. Mind you, if the players had been earning fifty grand a week, perhaps they would not have seen the funny side. It's the money that has kicked the laughter out of the game.

Clown Prince Len Shackleton was the creator of an even funnier penalty than Greavsie's corker against Gordon Banks. Shack was playing for Sunderland against Manchester City, who had the great Frank Swift in goal. He ran up and dummied as if to take the penalty. Swiftie dived for a ball that had not yet been kicked, and Shack calmly back-heeled it from the spot into the opposite corner of the net. Big Frank got up, charged after Shack as if he were in a wild temper, grabbed hold of him and gave his England team-mate a big kiss! They certainly don't make them like that any more.

Charlie 'Cannonball Shot' Wayman missed a second-minute penalty when playing for Newcastle against Newport County in a Second Division match at St James' Park on 5 October 1946. But few people could recall it at the end of a sensational game that finished Newcastle 13, Newport 0! Len Shackleton, making his Newcastle debut after being bought for what was then a whopping £13,500, helped himself to six goals.

In the last match of the season, Newcastle went to Newport for the return match, needing a win to clinch promotion. This time, they were beaten 4–2 by Newport, who were already doomed to relegation. It's an amazing old game.

I am sure there has never been a penalty quite like the one the great Johan Cruyff took for Ajax against Helmond Sports in 1982; and you will never see one like it again. He placed the ball on the spot, dummied as if to shoot, then passed the ball square to Jesper Olsen, who came running into the penalty area. Olsen returned the ball into the path of Cruyff, who directed it into the net, past a no-doubt cross-eyed goalkeeper. The reason I can be confident that we will never see this repeated is that the penalty dodge was quickly outlawed by FIFA (the ball now has to go forward from the spot).

Talking of outlawed techniques, how about the 'donkey kick' goal Ernie Hunt scored for Coventry against Everton in 1970? Willie Carr stood over the ball at a free-kick with the Everton wall in front of him. He wedged both feet around the ball and hooked it up like a donkey back-kicking. Hunt met it on the volley and the ball screamed into the roof of the net. It was wonderfully inventive, but the miserable lawmakers banned it, decreeing that a free-kick had to be taken with one foot. The bloody people running the game have as much imagination as flatulent, befuddled fleas.

Blackburn and England goalkeeper Tim Flowers liked to dig a marker divot in his goal area with his heel, so that he knew where he was in line with his posts. It boomeranged on him five minutes into a Premiership match against Liverpool at Ewood Park in 1996. Stan Collymore mishit a shot from twenty-five yards that was rolling towards Flowers, who went down on one knee to make what should have been an easy collection. The ball hit the divot that Flowers had dug and suddenly bounced high over his shoulder and into the net for the softest goal of Stan's career. Flowers wilted.

Peter Schmeichel was one of the best goalkeepers ever to play the game, but even he could become the victim of some lovely howlers. Probably the one that gave him the biggest embarrassment was when, playing for Man United, he shanked a clearance at a ninety-degree angle into the path of Barnsley striker John Hendrie in an FA Cup tie in 1998. Hendrie could not believe his luck as he steered the ball into the gaping net, with Schmeichel racing back towards the goal like a man chasing a mugger.

Alan Hudson spirited what became known as the 'ghost goal' for Chelsea against Ipswich at Stamford Bridge in 1970. He hammered the ball into the side-netting and was astonished to see referee Roy Capey pointing to the centre-circle to signal a goal that put Chelsea on the way to a 2–1 victory.

'I didn't argue with the ref,' said Hudson. 'You've got to be a bit stupid to protest if you're being awarded a goal.'

On the very same day at Filbert Street, Portsmouth forward Jim Storrie headed the ball wide of Leicester goalkeeper Peter Shilton. The ball hit the stanchion at the back of the net and bounced back into play. The referee waved play on, thinking the ball had hit the crossbar.

'I couldn't believe it,' said Shilton, after Leicester had won the match 2–0. 'The ball definitely went into the net, but my team-mates would have shot me if I'd chased after the ref and told him he should have given Portsmouth a goal.' This was from the man who was on the receiving end of the Hand of God some sixteen years later!

And how about Man United goalkeeper Roy Carroll, when television replays clearly showed him fielding the ball miles behind the United goal-line against Tottenham in a Premiership match in 2005? The referee and his assistant were right out of line on this one.

All of these incidents screamed out for the use of television technology to help sort out controversial decisions. The only thing that should matter is getting it right.

Terry Venables scored what must rate as the cheekiest goal at Stamford Bridge when playing for Chelsea against Roma in a 1965 Fairs Cup tie. Chelsea had been awarded a free-kick just outside the penalty area. Venables placed the ball as if he were going to take the kick and then made a great fuss of pacing out the stipulated ten yards, holding up his fingers in mime of a count as he approached the Roma wall of defenders.

The Italians, duped into thinking that our Tel was going to have to return to the ball, opened up the wall and allowed him through as he continued his count. Suddenly, Venables shouted to team-mate John Hollins, 'Give it now, John.' Hollins steered the ball through the hole in the middle of the wall and Venables coolly fired a low shot into the net for one of the three goals that he collected that night. *Mama mia*, or words to that effect!

Another Chelsea goal that caused great amusement – though not to scorer Tommy Harmer – came in a vital Second Division promotion match at Sunderland in 1963. Harmer, a Tom Thumb of a player nicknamed 'the

Charmer' because of his immaculate ball skills, said, 'Tears come to my eyes every time I recall that goal which won us the match and clinched promotion back to the First Division. There was an inswinging corner and the ball went into the net off what I can only describe as my private parts. It hurt like hell, but it was worth it.'

Tommy Docherty, Chelsea's manager at the time, said after the match that in future Harmer should be known as 'the cock of the north' or 'the man with the secret weapon'.

One of the funniest goals must have been the one scored by Fulham goalkeeper Frank Elliott against Plymouth at Home Park in 1954. Elliott was injured in a collision as he collected a cross. He attempted to throw the ball out of play so that he could receive treatment, but succeeded only in tossing it into his own net. Did Frank's injury hurt? Only when he laughed.

Headed goals can be just as spectacular as those scored with the feet. Take the one netted by Peter Aldis for Aston Villa against Sunderland in 1952, for instance. He sent it dipping into the net from thirty-five yards, one of the longest headed goals on record.

But surely the most astonishing headed goal ever seen in a League match was one by Arsenal and England skipper Eddie Hapgood. It has passed into folklore how he headed a goal from the penalty spot at Anfield in 1935. Eddie hammered in a spot-kick (with his boot) that was fisted out by the Liverpool goalkeeper. Still standing on the penalty spot, the Gooner promptly headed it into the net.

Eddie Baily was a Cockney 'cheeky chappie' in the immediate post-war years and made the famous push-and-run Spurs tick. He once created a goal with the assistance of a referee. His corner-kick hit the ref in the back, Eddie collected the rebound and chipped the ball to the far post, where Len Duquemin headed it home. There was a lot of argument that the referee should have ruled the goal illegal because Baily had, in effect, played the ball twice from a corner, but it was allowed to stand.

The best goalscorers always have a lot of self-confidence, but nobody had more of it than a young Middlesbrough centre-forward called Brian Clough. He was one of the most prolific hitmen of his generation before a knee injury forced his premature retirement. Early in his career at Middlesbrough a young winger complained to the manager that Cloughie – his team-mate – had knocked him off the ball in front of an open goal and scored himself just as the winger was shaping to shoot. When asked about the incident, Cloughie shrugged and told the manager in a matter-of-fact way, 'Well, I'm better at it than he is.' End of conversation.

David Seaman is a smashing bloke. I know because I have worked with him on a television show called *Ricky's Joke Shop*. He allowed me to take the pee out of him something rotten over that horror goal he conceded against Ronaldinho in the 2002 World Cup quarter-final against Brazil.

Pony-tailed Seaman, who is to hairstyles what Laurence Llewellyn-Bowen is to men's fashion, was beaten by a freakish free-kick that swung into the net from thirty-five yards out. We will never know whether Ronaldinho meant it, but we do know that the goal signalled an early exit for England and reduced Seaman (and many of his countrymen watching on the box) to tears.

'Even if I knew what he was going to do, I doubt I could have saved it,' honest David told me. 'It was one of those freak shots that swirled into the top corner. If it was a deliberate attempt to score, it was fantastic, but my gut feeling is that he meant it as a cross. What I do know is that it was the worst moment of my life.'

I had an in-depth discussion with David about the difference between the old leather football and today's characterless ball. He made the point that the modern ball swerves and swings much more than the old one, and that is why goalkeepers are caught out so many times by curling free-kicks.

He was not best pleased when – sensitive soul that I am – I said, 'Well, you would know all about that, David.'

David came on to *Joke Shop* pretending to be his own looka-like, and I threw him a video cassette that he caught. 'You can't be David Seaman,' I said. 'He would have dropped that.'

Goalkeepers of Seaman's class – and, let's be honest, he's one of the all-time greats – are often in the firing line against top-quality opponents. As a result, they can be made to look very foolish. They can either learn to laugh off the silly moments, or go mad.

David will not be best pleased when I point out that the Ronaldinho goal was a nightmare revisited. He was beaten by a similar long-range effort from Nayim in the last seconds of Arsenal's 1995 European Cup Winners' Cup final against Real Zaragoza. The joke that flew around the football world was: 'Who can lob semen from forty yards? Nayim!'

Nobody ever worked harder for a goal than Ian Storey-Moore when he was playing for Nottingham Forest against Everton in the sixth round of the FA Cup in 1967. The scores were level and the match was into its last minute when John Winfield and Frank Wignall combined to thread the ball through to Ian, who was fifteen yards from the Everton goal. He took a snap shot and the ball hit defender John Hurst. He collected the rebound and fired in a second shot that was pushed out by goalkeeper Andy Rankin. Storey-Moore then nodded the clearance against the crossbar, before dashing forward to head the ball into the net for a remarkable winning goal. Bloody hell, I'm knackered just describing it!

Manchester City were in possession deep in West Bromwich Albion's half in a First Division match in 1969. Colin Bell pushed the ball back to Mike Doyle, who in turn passed it back to City colleague Tommy Booth. He passed it back to skipper Tony Book, so the ball was now deep in City's half, without a West Brom player getting a sniff of it. Book then pushed the ball to goalkeeper Harry Dowd who threw it straight to the feet of West Brom striker Tony Brown, who struck it first time into the net.

Veteran manager Joe Mercer walked into the dressing-room after the match shaking his head in disbelief. 'Five effing passes to set up a goal for *them*,' he fumed. 'I've been in this game nearly fifty effing years, and I thought I had seen every way a goal could be scored, but today you have just found another permu-effing-tation.'

Here comes a comedy classic that was hilarious for everybody but those immediately involved in its creation. Grimsby were playing League Cup holders Leicester City in 1997 when a long cross was sent into the Leicester penalty area. Goalkeeper Kasey Keller elected to punch the ball, missed and connected with his team-mate Julian Watts, who went down for the count as if poleaxed. Grimsby forward Steve Livingstone fired the ball into the unattended net as Leicester defender Steve Walsh came sliding in with a death-or-glory clearance attempt. He missed the ball and slid into a post, collecting three broken ribs. So both Watts and Walsh were laid out in the penalty area and the ball was nestling in the back of the net. It's so funny it hurts.

Adelaide striker Damian Mori claims the fastest goal ever. Playing against Sydney in 1995, the ball was passed to him from the kick-off and he thundered it into the net from fifty-five yards. It was timed at 3.5 seconds. Mori later rejected a move to Manchester City, no doubt because he considered them too slow and plodding a side!

During a League match Port Vale goalkeeper Paul Musselwhite came charging out of the penalty box towards the right touchline, pushing the ball into touch. Quick-thinking Sheffield United striker Dean Saunders aimed an instant throw at the back of the retreating Musselwhite and curled the rebound into the net for a last-minute winner. There were the usual arguments as to whether it was legal, but the goal stood. Port Vale were completely thrown by it.

One of my biggest heroes when I was a new kid on the Kop at Anfield was a Geordie called Albert Stubbins. If he were playing today he would be a zillionaire. He scored more goals than anybody else during the wartime leagues (226 for Newcastle), and he had such a cannonball shot that he once broke a goalkeeper's arm with a penalty.

Our Albert was signed by Liverpool in competition with Everton, who saw him as the ideal number nine to follow the legends Dixie Dean and Tommy Lawton. When it was learned that he was prepared to leave Newcastle, negotiators rushed from Anfield and Goodison. The man representing the Reds was that little bit craftier. Albert was at the pictures when he arrived in Newcastle, and the artful Scouser had a message flashed up on the screen: 'Mr Albert Stubbins, go to the cinema manager's office immediately.'

Albert went on to score many picture goals for Liverpool, helping to shoot them to the League title in 1946–47 and to the 1950 FA Cup final at Wembley. It is burned into the memories of Anfield fans of a certain age how Albert dived full length on a snow-covered pitch to head in a Billy Liddell free-kick in an FA Cup tie against Birmingham.

But the legend does not end there. He has been captured for all time on the most famous of all The Beatles' record covers. Look closely at *Sergeant Pepper's Lonely Hearts Club Band* and you will find our Albert tucked in between George Bernard Shaw and transcendental guru Sri Lahiri Mahasaya. I preferred to follow the teachings of Albert: shoot first, ask questions later.

Talking of footballers captured for eternity . . . which

goalscoring master was fastest across the Atlantic on water? Answer: Steve Bloomer, who was featured in a huge mural on the old *Queen Mary* that set a transatlantic-crossing record in 1936. Not a lot of people know that!

If there was an award for the Goal of the Twentieth Century, I think it would have to go to Celtic's Patsy Gallagher. Playing against Dundee in the 1925 Scottish Cup final at Hampden Park, 'Mighty Atom' Gallagher dribbled past five defenders before he was sent crashing with a tackle five yards from the goal. As he fell, he managed to lodge the ball between his feet and somersaulted with the ball into the net. It was the sort of circus-trick goal that might have broken today's action-replay machines.

Celtic had another scorer of unusual goals in Charlie Tully, an Irishman full of tantalising trickery. His speciality was scoring from inswinging corners. In one Scottish League match he sent the ball swerving into the net but was ordered to retake the kick because the referee had not been ready. So Charlie produced a carbon copy of the first corner, the ball swinging into the exact same place in the net. Charlie had them cornered.

My particular favourite goal of recent years came in the Euro '96 championships that were staged in England. It deserves a full description, including the build-up to the match.

The England team managed by Terry Venables came into the tournament under a cloud of controversy after some of their drink-fuelled players had got involved in a wild night out in Hong Kong following a match that was meant to warm them up for the championship action at home. Paul Gascoigne, who often went a prank too far, was again at the centre of it all. He and several team-mates were photographed pouring drinks down one another's throats while half-lying in a pseudo dentist's chair in a nightclub. Then, on the flight home, several players were accused of causing

Gazza is as daft as a brush but lovely with it. He told me that while he was playing in China he ate duck's head, chicken's feet, bat's wings and pigeon's eyes. 'I was able to fly home without a plane,' he said with that maniacal grin of his. He was the most gifted footballer of his generation.

damage to airline property. It was bad enough having fans as hooligans; now the players were behaving like louts.

Only an exceptional performance in the championships could restore their pride and self-respect. And that was exactly what they produced under the influence – I almost said *intoxicating* influence – of master coach Venables.

England were held 1–1 by Switzerland in the opening game at Wembley, a harsh penalty awarded against Stuart Pearce cancelling out an Alan Shearer goal and costing them a deserved victory.

Then came the 'British final' – England against Scotland, who had held Holland to a goalless draw in their first game. It was a cracker.

Trailing 1–0 to a Shearer goal, the Scots were awarded a penalty twelve minutes from the end. David Seaman saved superbly from Gary McAllister, and within a minute the one and only Gazza had scored a gem of a second goal for England. He cleverly chipped the ball over the head of his Rangers clubmate Colin Hendry, collected it on its way down and found the net with an exquisite shot. It was a goal in the Pele class.

But the bit that earned the goal a place in my funny-goals collection was the celebration after it. 'Daft-as-a-brush' Gazza – Bobby Robson's nickname for him – sprinted to a chosen spot at the side of the Scottish goal, and as he lay down England teammates poured bottled water down his throat in a send-up of the dentist's chair incident. The crowd loved it, and suddenly the England players were forgiven their boisterous behaviour in Hong Kong.

It drives me potty to see goal celebrations often taking longer than the move that created the goal itself. Remember, I am from the generation that grew up watching our idols Billy Liddell, Tommy Lawton and Tom Finney scoring goals and then jogging back to the centre-circle with just a pat from one or two teammates. Now we are continually treated to near-rape scenes. But on this occasion I thought the England boys got their celebration spot on. It was a great parody, and almost as well thought out as the magnificent goal.

Yes, Mr Venables, it was as good as an orgasm.

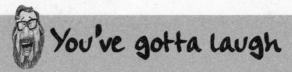# You've gotta laugh

Three ancient football fans are praying alongside each other in church. One wears an England scarf, the second an Everton scarf and the third a Manchester United scarf.

The first one, his eyes tightly closed, asks, 'Oh Lord God Almighty, please tell me when England will next win the World Cup?'

God replies, 'It will be at least another eight years.'

The old man shakes his head as he says sadly, 'But I'll most likely be dead by then.'

The second fan puts his hands together and asks, 'Oh Lord God Almighty, please tell me when Everton will win the Premiership?'

God replies, 'This, I am afraid, will take more than ten years.'

The ageing supporter fingers his Everton scarf lovingly and says, 'I will probably not be alive to see it.'

The Manchester United fan puts his hands together, and asks, 'Oh Lord God Almighty, please tell me when Malcolm Glazer will have paid off the debts incurred buying my beloved club?'

God answers, 'I'll be dead long before then.'

Hark who's talking

Ian Rush:
'I just couldn't settle in Italy. It was like living in a foreign country.'

Thierry Henry:
'If the referee had eyes, he would have sent Neville off.'

Kevin Keegan:
'Lineker always weighed up his options, especially when he had no choice.'

David Unsworth:
'Wayne Rooney can go all the way to the top if he keeps his head firmly on the ground.'

Sir Alex Ferguson:
'Andy Cole should be scoring from those distances, but I'm not going to single him out.'

Steve Bruce:
'The only English I ever understood from Eric Cantona was "Goal!"'

Frank Worthington:
'I had eleven clubs, or twelve if you count Stringfellows.'

Tommy Docherty:
'Tony Hateley had it all. The only thing he lacked was ability.'

Rodney Marsh:
'I told our new manager that we are all behind him fifty per cent.'

John Toshack:
'Ruud Gullit had everything, apart from a short back and sides.'

Alan Shearer:
'I've never wanted to leave. I'm here for the rest of my life, and hopefully after that as well.'

Stan Collymore:
'I faxed a transfer request to the club at the beginning of the week, but let me state that I don't want to leave Leicester.'

Tommy Lawton:
'I am in it for the money, but I am not mercenary.'

Peter Osgood:
'Alf Ramsey is a great coach but like all great coaches he doesn't want you to think for yourself.'

Nat Lofthouse:
'I saw my job as putting the ball into the net, and if I took the goalkeeper in as well, that was all part and parcel of the game.'

Frank Worthington:
'If I had scored as many times on the pitch as I did off it, I would have been up there with Pele.'

Dixie Dean:
'I'm being treated in a ward for people who have lost their legs. It looks as if Tommy Smith has been let loose in here.'

Allan Clarke:
'I don't know why they call me Sniffer, apart from the fact that I sniff out goals.'

Len Shackleton:
'I once accidentally sat on the ball in the goalmouth, and didn't know whether to put it into the net or hatch it.'

Mike Channon:
'Sex comes a poor third to scoring a winning goal and saddling a winning horse.'

Bill Shankly:
'He [a well known international] scores lots of goals despite having a heart the size of a caraway seed.'

Martin Chivers:
'Our coach Eddie Baily shouts like mad on the touchline, and we can't hear a thing out in the middle. All you can see is Eddie's mouth opening and closing, mostly in the f-word shape. It's like watching Tower Bridge open and close.'

Rodney Marsh:
'It's the best goal I've ever scored . . . almost as good as the one I scored in the League Cup final at Wembley.'

Alan Shearer:
'One accusation you can't throw at me is that I've always done my best.'

Thierry Henry:
'Sometimes in football you have to score goals.'

Les Ferdinand:
'I was surprised, but I always say nothing surprises me in football.'

3 Footballers' Wives

Footballers' wives used to be as anonymous as ladies-in-waiting at Buckingham Palace. You knew they were there in the background, but could not begin to put a name to them. Then along came Posh and Becks, with their Beckingham Palace and swanky 'superstar' lifestyle, and suddenly the marriages and match-making of the players began to claim as much attention as their match performances.

Wearing my Mike Bassett hat, if my missus flashed her assets in public, I would strangle her with her knicker elastic. Mike is out of the old school, believing that footballers' – and managers' – wives should neither be seen nor heard. For example, he turned down a mega-money offer to pose with his wife for pictures in their prefab home for the magazine *Goodbye!* And they told the *KO!* photographer where to stick his camera.

Thinking back to the great Liverpool team of the 1960s, I can say, hand on heart, that I cannot tell you the name of any of the players' wives. Today, hand on wallet, the wives have a far higher profile, and in some cases overshadow their husbands. I can borrow the lovely description I heard of a US Ryder Cup golfer, who was said to be 'overwifed' – meaning that she wore the trousers. Blimey, at least he is not like Beckham, getting himself photographed wearing a skirt; or having his wife say in public that he likes to wear her panties. Hear that clanking and screaming? That's Bill Shankly rotating in his grave.

The funniest – or perhaps the most frightening – case of a footballer's wife scoring, so to speak, was when England midfielder Ray Parlour took a kick in the bank balance. When he was divorced from Karen, his wife of seven years, the initial settlement was two mortgage-free houses worth £1 million plus a £250,000 lump sum. But there were bigger lumps to come that really bruised Ray in the wallet. He was ordered by the Court of Appeal to cough up a personal maintenance of £406,500 a year to his ex-wife until the end of his playing career, when there would be a review of the situation. Ray got as far away from his Arsenal roots as possible – to Middlesbrough – knowing that his former missus was still on the gravy train with him.

Footballers – and their wives – are often portrayed as thick, greedy and self-centred, which in the majority of cases is neither fair nor accurate. But there are footballers who have their brains in their boots, and I am reminded of the joke about the Premiership player who sneaks off early from a training session while the manager is away. He hurries home for some nookie with his wife, and he is astonished when he gets to their mansion to find parked in the drive his manager's Mercedes. Tiptoeing quietly, he goes to the bedroom window and sees the manager and his wife locked in the friendliest of embraces. Then he tiptoes back to his car and drives off in a state of shock.

The next day at training the manager is again missing. 'You going to nip off early again?' a team-mate asks.

'No bloody fear,' says our hero. 'I almost got caught yesterday.'

Posh and Becks have done most to inspire the footballers' wives culture, sitting on thrones at their wedding reception, flashing their fashions and jewellery for all to see, and having their agenda largely controlled by media managers. They have been leading their lives in a golden goldfish bowl. Good luck to them, I say, but it really got up my nostrils when Posh – or surely her advisers – went for the jugular because little Peterborough United

David Beckham is surprised to find the referee is a Spice Girls fan as he suddenly breaks into a chorus of 'I'll tell ya what I want, what I really, really want . . .' David advises him to stick to his day job.

were trying to register Posh as their nickname. Bloody hell, they have been Posh since I was knee high to a Subbuteo footballer, and they had the nickname long before Victoria Beckham had her first whiff of the Essex estuary.

Lawyers acting for Mrs Beckham – who has certainly put a lot of spice into her marriage to Becks – blocked a Peterborough bid to turn 'Posh' into a registered trademark, which was designed to help them in their day-to-day struggle for survival in the financial jungle that is football these days. Her publicist issued a pompous statement that read, 'The name "Posh" is inexorably associated with Victoria Beckham in the public's mind, and the concern is that the public would think she had in some way endorsed products she had no knowledge of.' Peterborough United supporters made it clear that they hated the idea of their Posh merchandise linking them in any way with the ex-Spice Girl. After three months it was announced that Victoria's stance on the subject had 'moderated significantly', and that Peterborough could continue to be called the Posh. How generous of her, to let them keep a name they've been using since the dawn of the twentieth century. It was appalling PR and, in football speak, Posh had scored a shocking own goal.

Talking of the Beckhams (whom I love dearly, really), here just for laughs, is a collection of Posh and Becks jokes that came my way when I let it be known I was looking for funny football stories.

Becks goes home to Posh after training with his Real Madrid team-mates.

'How did it go today, Babes?' asks Posh.

'Weren't bad,' says David. 'But Michael Owen got up me nose a bit. He's asked if he can have a cortisone injection before Sunday's match. Who the bloody hell does he think he is? Only been here five minutes and already he's making demands.'

'You're not going to stand for that sort of favouritism, are you?' says an indignant Posh.

'No way,' says David. 'If he's going to have a cortisone injection, then I'm going to demand one of them new Aston Martins.'

Posh and Becks are sitting together in front of the television watching the ten o'clock Sky news on their plasma-screen satellite TV in Madrid. The top story features a man threatening to jump off the top of Tower Bridge into the Thames.

Posh says, 'David, I bet you a new diamond ring that he jumps into the water.'

'You're on,' says David. 'If he jumps, I'll buy you a diamond ring. If he don't jump, you buy me a new diamond earring stud.'

Just as he finishes speaking the man jumps into the Thames.

'Oh bum,' says David. 'That's fifty grand I've got to fork out for a new ring for you.'

Posh cuddles him. 'I can't go through with it, Babes,' she says. 'I was cheating. I knew he jumped because I saw it on the five o'clock news.'

'No, Babe,' says David. 'You won the bet fair and square 'cos I was also cheating. I saw the earlier news, too, but I didn't think the idiot would be stupid enough to go and do it again.'

Becks goes shopping in a Madrid department store and is intrigued by a brightly coloured flask on show in the kitchen department. He takes out his Spanish phrasebook and asks the assistant, 'Is what that?'

'Señor Beckham,' says the assistant, 'I speak perfect English. May I say that you are my favourite footballer.'

'Course you can say it,' says David.

'Señor,' says the assistant, 'what can I help you with?'

'Like I said in Spanish,' says David, pointing to the flask. 'What is that?'

'Ah,' replies the assistant. 'That is a Thermos flask.'

'Really,' says Becks. 'What does it do?'

The assistant explains how it keeps hot things hot and cold things cold.

'I must have one,' says David.

'Señor, please have it on the store,' insists the assistant. 'In return, please try to score a goal for us on Sunday.'

Beckham takes the flask home to Posh. 'Look what I've been given, Victoria,' he says proudly. 'It's a Thermos flask.'

Posh is impressed. 'What does it do, Babes?'

'It keeps hot things hot and cold things cold,' says David.

'What a clever thing,' says Posh. 'And what have you got in it?'

'Two cups of coffee,' says David, 'and a strawberry ice lolly.'

Becks is celebrating, running around the lounge of their Spanish villa, punching the air. 'I've done it,' he shouts, as excited as if he has just scored one of his spectacular free-kicks. 'I've finished.'

'Finished what, Babes?' asks Posh, peering up from the sunbed.

'I've completed this jigsaw puzzle,' says Becks. 'And in record time.'

'How d'you know it's a record, Babes?'

'Well, it's only taken me forty-seven days,' he says proudly. 'On the box it says three to five years.'

It was reported in the Spanish press that David Beckham had a narrow escape from serious injury when he went riding at the weekend. Everything was apparently going fine until the horse started bucking out of control. He tried desperately to hang on but it was no good. With his foot trapped in the stirrup, he went head-first over the horse's neck and crashed to the floor. His head continued to bump on the ground as the horse refused to stop or even slow down.

Panic-stricken Posh ran for help, crying as she went. 'I told him he should have worn a hard hat,' she said over and over again.

The papers reported a happy ending. Just as Becks was giving up hope and losing consciousness, Posh came back with the store manager, who managed to unplug the horse.

On a serious note, I wish to state here and now that Becks is one of the greatest English-born footballers of my lifetime, and if he had a left foot as good as his right he would be up there challenging the finest footballers of all time. He and Posh get the pee taken out of them something rotten, but that's what happens when you put yourself up there on a pedestal. Becks is there to be shot at, but the bottom line is that he can't half play the game.

Here's a quite moving anecdote that dear old Joe Mercer used to tell that captures how the lives of footballers and their wives have changed. It's close to my heart because it involves a Scouser who was born in Scotland Road in Liverpool, and you can't get more Scouse than that. It's like a Londoner being born in the Old Kent Road, or a Glaswegian first seeing the light of day in Sauchiehall Street. This is how Joe told it:

Jimmy Dugdale was one of the most likeable characters I ever had the pleasure of managing. He was a bit of a scally but very quick-witted and a former college student who was bright academically as well as possessing a good football brain. He won FA Cup winners' medals with West Brom and Aston Villa, and it was when I became Villa manager that I discovered what a lovely bloke he was. He was married to a girl called Dot from Tipton.

They were a smashing couple and very much in love, but they used to fight like cat and dog. And I do mean fight. I remember returning to Villa from a scouting trip to find that Jimmy had been missing from training. My trainer Ray Shaw reported, 'The Dugdales are at it again!'

There was an important cup match to be played that night – a Wednesday – and Jimmy hadn't been seen since the previous Saturday. Nobody would volunteer to go round the Dugdales' house, they were that frightened of Dot when she was in one of her tempers.

So, being the manager, I accepted that it was my duty to go to see them and get things sorted out. It's all part and parcel of a manager's life. Off I went to see them, and with some trepidation because things were liable to fly! I can even remember their address, I was there that often – 60 Corporation Street. I took a deep breath and rat-a-tat-tatted on their door.

Jimmy opened the door immediately. He was looking as smart and debonair as usual, but I could tell something was wrong. 'Hello, Boss,' he said as friendly and as matter of fact as if I had called round for a game of cards. 'Come on in.'

As I followed him into the lounge he said over his shoulder, 'We've just had a slight domestic upheaval.'

Then Dot appeared. 'D'you take sugar with your tea, Mr Mercer?' she asked.

What could I do but laugh? Here they were acting as if nothing had happened when I knew they'd been going at it hammer and tongs since the weekend.

The punchline is that we won the match and Jimmy played a blinder. The lads invited him out for a celebratory drink, and *he said – making us all collapse – 'No f***ing chance. Dot would cut the other bollock off!'*

For the first time in the book I am into the dodgy territory where I have to start changing names to protect the guilty and to keep the bites-yer-leg lawyers at bay. I have found some smashing, true husband-and-wife stories involving top players, but they will have to be told on the old hush-hush.

Fairly recently, there was an England international on Merseyside who had a wife with a tongue that could kill at six paces. If ever she felt her husband was being wronged, she would let rip. After he had been dropped to the substitutes' bench one week she stormed into the manager's office and gave him a right bollocking at the top of her voice.

Finally, the manager got a word in. 'Look, he *asked* to be rested,' he explained. 'He said you had nagged him so much through the previous night that he was tired out.'

Exit speechless wife.

Bill McGarry, former manager of Wolves and Ipswich, revealed that he used to hide under his desk when he heard the wife of one of his players on the warpath in the outer office. 'She used to frighten the life out of me,' he said. 'If ever I left her husband out she would come storming after me like a bat out of hell.' Sounds as if he should have selected *her*.

Not so long ago, the wife of a player with a London club came home early from the hairdresser's to find her husband in bed . . . with one of his team-mates! She grabbed a carving knife and stabbed him in the arse. He had to have stitches in the wound and missed a couple of games. When the manager found out he felt really stitched up, and the player was sold soon after.

At another southern club, the chairman's wife bedded the manager. They had just finished their, um, training session when she calmly picked up the bedside telephone, rang her husband and said, 'I have just f***ed your manager.'

The chairman considered his situation, decided it would be more expensive to get rid of his wife, so sacked the manager, who later became extremely successful with a northern club.

The most high-profile club-affair case was when Tommy Docherty ran off with Mary Brown, the Old Trafford physiotherapist's wife, while manager of Manchester United. The story hit the headlines just a few weeks after the Doc had led United to the FA Cup final victory over Liverpool in 1977. The United fans gleefully sang 'Knees up Mother Brown' from the terraces.

No, it's not the Kaiser. It's Tommy Docherty celebrating Man United's 1977 FA Cup final victory over Liverpool at Wembley. A few weeks later the Doc was sacked for running off with the club physiotherapist's wife. He rubbed him up the wrong way.

Copyright © popperfoto.com

Tommy, who can see humour in any situation, said, 'I was sacked for falling in love. One of the United supporters came up to me and said if I could win the championship, he'd let me run off with *his* wife!'

And what sort of heartaches did the Brazilian wing wizard Garrincha give to his two wives and many mistresses? He fathered thirteen children, ten of them girls, and his affairs included the partner of his club's vice-president along with nightclub dancers and singers. It's a wonder he found time to play football as well as anybody else in history. His talent was not confined to the pitch. It was claimed that, though quite small in stature, he was extremely well endowed in another area. His many daughters tried to sue the writer who revealed this fact following his untimely death at the age of forty-nine, claiming that it was demeaning to his memory. The judge said in his summing up that 'a large penis was a reason for pride not melancholy' and that it made Garrincha even more of a hero in the eyes of Brazilian men. The case was kicked out, so his daughters had made a right cock-up of that.

How about this for a shock for a footballer's wife: when she finds out her husband prefers to live as a woman? It happened to the wife of a footballer in the old First Division, who apparently wore her clothes better than she did. I will spare their blushes by not naming names, but he was well known to spectators in East Anglia and when last heard of was running a motel in the United States with his male partner and talking of having a sex-change op.

Milene Dominguez, the ex-wife of Brazilian World Cup star Ronaldo, could keep balls in the air longer than her husband. She played for the Fiamma Monza club and in 1997 set a world record for keepy-uppies at 55,187 juggles without the ball touching the ground.

Footballers' wives are notoriously protective of their husbands when watching them play, and there are many instances of them getting involved in slanging matches with spectators having a go at their man. Judith Hurst was infamous for standing up for her World Cup hero Geoff, and it was rumoured that she whacked a loud-mouthed critic with her handbag. I wonder if she hit him three times for a hat-trick?

These days a club has to keep the wife as well as her footballing husband happy when they are signing a new player. David Unsworth, for instance, had been at Aston Villa for just a week when his wife made it clear she would not leave Liverpool to live in the Midlands (good judge). So Villa were forced to sell Unsworth to Everton. 'He told me he didn't realise how far Birmingham was from Liverpool', said perplexed Villa manager John Gregory.

When Alan Mullery became the first player sent off wearing an England shirt in the 1968 European championships in Italy he phoned home and received a terrible ear-bashing from his wife, June. 'She told me I have let the country and the family down, and that I was a disgrace,' he said. 'Blimey, it was almost as bad as being sent off.'

A couple of years later Mullery literally went into battle for his wife. She was insulted by a yob supporter, who pushed her in the car park as he tried to get to her husband after a Tottenham defeat. The Spurs midfielder took off his jacket and gave the thug a good hiding. Good for him. 'He could call me what he liked,' said Mullery, 'but nobody insults my wife and gets away with it.'

Jimmy Greaves tells a story of how his Tottenham and England team-mate Bobby Smith went missing on the morning of the 1962 FA Cup final against Burnley at Wembley. 'We were just thinking about sending out a search party for him,' recalls Greavsie, 'when he appeared back at the hotel just before we were due to climb on the coach for the short trip to the stadium. I asked him where the hell he'd been, and he told me matter of factly that he had gone to do the Saturday-morning shopping for his wife! He lived in north London and found the time to shop and then run the groceries home.'

In these days of mega-money pay packets, we tend to forget that it was not too long ago that footballers were considered 'soccer slaves' who were restricted to a maximum wage of twenty pounds a week. 'Wor' Jackie Milburn, idol of Tyneside, told this story that captures the meanness of clubs in those good old, bad old days:

Newcastle would never go in for the under-the-counter payments like other clubs. But, sitting in the dressing-room after the third of our three FA Cup final victories at Wembley in the 1950s, we were led to understand that at the celebration dinner and dance our wives would be presented with handbags. We were told the news with a lot of winking and keep-it-secret, fingers-to-the-lips signals. This convinced us the bags would be stuffed full of money, and when we whispered it to our wives they got as excited as we were.

We could hardly wait to open the bags as our wives went up one by one to receive them as if they were being presented with FA Cup winners' medals. They looked to be bulging, and as one of the wives returned to the table the strap on the bag broke. We took that as a sign of the weight of the money.

As each of us pulled open the bags in eager anticipation we thought they were full of lovely white fivers. But it turned out to be tissue paper, and soon balls of it were decorating the dance floor as we rummaged for money that was not there. We did not get a pound note between us. Players and wives sat disconsolately at the side of the dance floor up to our ankles

*in scattered tissue paper. Suddenly none of us were in the
mood for dancing.*

*To rub it in, we later found out through a contact in the club
office that a Newcastle director had bought the bags as a job lot
for twenty quid!*

Our Merseyside watch, of course, takes in the antics of the boy wonder,
Wayne Rooney. Goodness knows what sort of marriage he will have
with his feisty fiancée Coleen McLoughlin, who looks to be a stereotype
footballer's wife in the making. How will she handle the off-pitch behaviour of a lad naïve enough to sign autographs while visiting a run-down
Liverpool brothel? The mind, as they say, boggles. But what a footballer!

Do you realise how dangerous it can be sleeping with a footballer?
Brenda Thomas once had a front tooth knocked out by her husband Dave, the former Everton and England winger, who was
throwing his arms around while dreaming of a match in which he
was playing.

I could name several current Liverpool imports who play as if
they're sleepwalking.

Howard Kendall is a smashing bloke, and he became a good friend
when he was managing Everton. He tells the story of how the stresses
of the job made him start looking to the bottom of a glass for a solu-
tion. It was not a very well-kept secret that Howard developed a drink
problem, and this caused a lot of friction at home. Everton, whom he
had guided to a string of sensational successes in his first stint as
manager at Goodison, hit a bad run. This, of course, made him drink
even more.

One day he drove home to his beautiful house in Formby to find that
sombeody had daubed 'KENDALL MUST GO' on his garage doors. The
next weekend Everton lost yet again, and when he got home – much later

than he had said he would – a word had been added to the garage door message: 'KENDALL MUST GO NOW'.

'I was fuming to think that fans were vandalising my home,' Howard said later. 'Then I found out that the word had been added by my wife!'

She was soon his ex-wife, and I am glad to report that Howard has kicked the bottle and is happily married the second time around.

Jamie Redknapp and his wife Louise come across as a much more balanced and stable couple than Posh and Becks. We on Merseyside have watched their love grow and their marriage strengthen with more interest than most because Jamie was a player at Anfield when he walked off with the lovely Louise. I had to chuckle when I saw this quote from Louise, when she was asked whether a number-one album or an FA Cup-winning goal would give her most satisfaction. 'What a cruel question,' she said. 'If I say the album, I will come across as very selfish. If I say the goal, it will make people think I lack ambition. So how about a number-one single for me and a goal for Jamie in the FA Cup final. But not the winner, provided his team take the Cup.'

Spoken like a true footballer's wife. Bread buttered on both sides, please!

The first headline-hitting football/showbiz marriage was long before Jamie and Louise came on the scene. Back in 1959, England captain Billy Wright married Joy Beverley, the one in the middle of the Beverley Sisters. It was Posh and Becks in black and white. There were no thrones, no banquets and no *Hello!* photographers for Billy and Joy. They tried to get married in secret at a register office in Poole, but it was leaked to the press and more than ten thousand people packed into the Dorset town to see them. Billy, the first footballer in the world to win a hundred caps, was earning twenty pounds a week at the time as captain of Wolves, and throughout his twenty-year playing career earned less than Becks picks up in a week. Blimey, just the thought of it would be enough to make Posh lose her voice.

Here's a little fact that might explain why so many footballers are, as they say, babe magnets. In 2004 alone, David Beckham earned £24 million.

You've gotta laugh

Arsène Wenger is desperate to find out how Jose Mourinho coaches Chelsea, so he gets the Portuguese manager to invite him along to one of his training sessions. He watches closely from the touchline but sees nothing that Arsenal don't do in their workouts.

When they break for lunch, Wenger quietly asks Mourinho how he gets his players so razor-sharp with their reflexes.

'I train them mentally as well as physically,' the Chelsea boss explains. 'I keep them on their toes by asking them tough questions that make them think deeply. This keeps them mentally sharp and alert. Let me give you an example.'

He calls over his skipper John Terry and sets him a teaser. 'John,' he says, 'he is not your brother, but still he is your father's son. Who is he?'

Like lightning, John replies, 'Easy-peasy. Of course, that is me.'

Mourinho pats John on the back and sends him away. 'You see, Arsène,' he says. 'That's the way to keep them sharp.'

Wenger decides to try it out the next day in training. He

summons Freddie Ljungberg to join him. 'Freddie, I have a question for you,' he says.

'Fire away, Boss.'

'Right, Freddie,' says Wenger, 'he is not your brother, but still he is your father's son. Who is he?'

Freddie blows out his cheeks, runs his hand through his hair and thinks hard and long. 'Can I have time to consider this one?' he asks. 'It's a bit early in the day for a tough teaser like this.'

Wenger gives him until the end of the training session to come up with the answer.

Freddie craftily calls skipper Patrick Vieira to one side and puts the question to him: 'He is not your brother, but still he is your father's son. Who is he?'

Vieira says without hesitation, 'That's obvious. It's me.'

At the end of the workout, Wenger summons Freddie to him. 'Well, have you worked it out?' he asks.

'Yes,' says Freddie, full of confidence. 'The answer is Patrick Vieira.'

Wenger throws his arms up in frustration. 'You dummy,' he says. 'The correct answer is John Terry.'

Hark who's talking

Kevin Keegan:
'I don't think they're as good as they are.'

Joe Royle:
'That was clearly a tackle aimed at getting revenge – or maybe it was just out-and-out retribution.'

Sir Bobby Robson:
'For a player to ask for a transfer has opened everybody's eyebrows.'

Malcolm Allison:
'We beat them 5–0, and they were lucky to get nil.'

Glenn Hoddle:
'Football is about ninety minutes on the day; it's about tomorrows really.'

Stuart McCall:
'To be second with one game to go – you can't ask for more.'

Dave Jones:
'I don't read everything I read in the press.'

Martin O'Neill:
'The best thing for them to do is to stay at 0–0 until they score the goal.'

Walter Smith:
'If we'd won, it would have meant an historic double-treble. But we weren't even thinking about that.'

Brian Clough:
'Football hooligans? Well, there are ninety-two club chairmen for a start.

Then there are the MPs in the House of Commons.'

Brian Little:
'We gained more from the game than they did . . . except they got the points.'

Bryan Robson:
'And at the end of the season you can only do as well as what you have done.'

Andy Roxburgh:
'Hagi is a brilliant player, but we're not going to get psychedelic over him.'

Peter Taylor:
'It should be a good match because they're a good football team as well and we're a good football team. It should be a very good match.'

Chris Coleman:
'If I am a manager and we won 5–1, I couldn't care if I have got aliens on the pitch. I don't care – look, it is 5–1.'

Walter Smith:
'The main thing in a cup tie is to get through.'

Howard Wilkinson:
'Once Tony Daley opens his legs you've got a problem.'

Lawrie McMenemy:
'Some of the players never dreamed they'd be playing at Wembley, but here they are today fulfilling those dreams.'

Alan Buckley:
'We didn't look like scoring, although we looked like we were going to get a goal.'

Terry Neill:
'I'm not superstitious or anything like that, but I'll just hope we'll play our best and put it in the laps of the gods.'

Arsène Wenger:
'Davor has a left leg and a nose in the box.'

Bill Shankly:
'Aye, it was 0–0, but we murdered them.'

Colin Todd:
'As we say in football, it'll go down to the last wire.'

Ian Holloway:
'Every dog has its day and today is woof-woof day. Today I want to celebrate promotion by barking.'

Brian Laws (Spying on Chelsea at Stamford Bridge before his Scunthorpe team met them in a 2005 FA Cup tie):
'The only weakness I've spotted is that they serve cold pies.'

Alan Buckley:
'The boy's feet have been up in the clouds since the win.'

Terry Venables:
'If history is going to repeat itself, I think we could expect the same thing again.'

Sir Alf Ramsay:
'If we had beaten Poland 10–1 in the 1974 World Cup qualifier it would have been a fair reflection of the play. The fact that we only drew 1–1 was beyond belief. I saw Ipswich chairman John Cobbold after the match and he described it as more one-sided than Custer's Last Stand.'

4 Jeepers Keepers

They say that all goalkeepers are crazy, and I've collected loads of evidence to support the case for the prosecution. If some of the goalies featured in this chapter were called to defend themselves, you could bet they'd drop themselves right in it!

I am a fully paid-up member of the goalkeepers' union. That was my chosen position after I got too bulky and breathless to motor around the midfield, my territory when I was a promising footballer as a youngster. My love of playing the game started with kick-abouts in the Liverpool streets, using coat jackets and jumpers for goalposts (and this was years before *The Fast Show*!). While John Lennon and Paul McCartney were starting to pluck their strings, I was getting stuck in on the wing. I'd have been as good as that Wayne Rooney kid if only I'd had a stronger left and right foot. My handicap was flat feet. If they'd been any flatter I could have skied to school without skis. My mam used to make me wear specially fitted leather shoes with wedge heels. I could really give out welly with them shoes on, and defenders in our street games got many a whack in the shins from Terror Tomlinson.

I always used to pretend I was Billy Liddell and would run like the bloody wind. Trouble was, with my shooting, I was more Piddle than Liddell: couldn't hit a barn door from ten paces. Mind you, I was pretty proud of one goal. We played in-off rules in our games in narrow Lance Street where I grew up in Liverpool, and I remember deliberately kicking the ball against the door of number eight, then taking the rebound and crashing it on the volley between the jackets. The old girl at number eight was not best pleased. But for me it was like scoring the winner at Wembley. I went bananas and ran the length of the street, a bit like Ian St John when he scored the extra-time winner for Liverpool against Leeds in 1965 to win the FA Cup for the Reds for the first time in their history. OK, I am exaggerating a bit, but I was pretty pleased with that rare goal of mine and treasure the memory. By the time I am ninety I will no doubt be describing how I played the ball off every door in Lance Street before banging it into the goal. That's the beauty of footie. It makes dreamers and schemers of us all.

I progressed to junior and youth matches on the Stanley Park public pitches, with the luxury of proper goalposts. Many's the time we'd kick the ball on to the adjoining pitch and see it go through the wrong posts, or have to threaten to fight to get our ball back from players in the other matches. Sometimes we'd get a ball kicked back to us only to discover it was not a patch on the one we'd started with. The crafty gits on the other pitch had made a switch. And the balls in them days! It was like heading a bloody brick. I am reliably informed that they weighed an ounce less than the beach balls they play with today, but those old leather foot-balls – with a lace that stuck out like corrugated spaghetti – were not water resistant and would often weigh twice as much by the end of a game played in mud.

Whenever I look across a deserted Stanley Park these days I can hear the shouts of our youth echoing from the past, bringing with it warm memories of when the world was young and the only cares you had were whether you were going to get the better of the scallies facing you on the pitch. It was our Anfield, our Goodison, our Wembley, our Hampden, our Maracana all wrapped into one. And to think that this is where the New Anfield will stand, right where I had my greatest footballing triumphs before health problems kicked me out of the game.

As my weight increased I found my breath decreasing, and I used to sound like a collapsing accordion as I fought for air. I was getting brought to my knees by the chronic bloody asthma that had troubled me since I was a kid. Every time I phoned our manager to tell him I couldn't make it for the weekend match he used to think he had a heavy breather on the blower, and would tell me to pee off. If it was his missus who answered, she'd let me reverse the charges. Only joking. So, literally breathlessly, I went farther down the team until I finished up in goal as a poacher turned 'keeper.

I played a lot of matches in those days at St George's Hill, which is the highest point in Liverpool. We felt like Edmund Hillary and the sherpas climbing the hill to the pitch each week, and were in need of oxygen by the time the game started. Our team was nicknamed Windy House, not because of the gales that often blew around the pitch but because we played like a lot of old farts. There was a great Wolves and England goalkeeper of the time called Bert 'the Cat' Williams. My team-mates also called me 'the Cat', but only because I gave them kittens.

My dad encouraged and coached me because he'd been a good goalie in his day, and had loads of tales about the golden oldies like Elisha Scott and Ted Sagar, who were both legends on

'Fingers' Tomlinson in his peak goalkeeping years in the 1960s. My team-mates called me Cinderella, because I was always late for the ball. At least I didn't look a tosser with a ponytail like that David Seaman, and Ronaldinho never beat me from forty yards. Mind you, I did often get beaten from four yards.

Copyright © E. Tomlinson

Merseyside. Scott was a larger-than-life Ulsterman with hands like spades, and he was as agile and quick as a cat in an aviary. He played more than five hundred games for Liverpool between the wars after doing the unthinkable ... moving to Anfield from Goodison. It has gone down in Liverpudlian footballing legend that after one stunning save against Blackburn a Kopite ran on to the pitch and kissed him full on the mouth. Some recent goal-keepers at Anfield have looked more in need of the kiss of life.

Elisha's big rival on Merseyside was the one and only Dixie Dean, the Everton headmaster who once scored sixty First Division goals in a single season. I'll repeat that: sixty goals in one season. Bloody hell, that's more than entire teams score today. The story handed down by my dad is that when Dixie met Elisha in Scotland Road he nodded a good morning to the Irishman, who instinctively dived into the gutter with his arms outstretched. Nonsense, of course, but it conjures a wonderful picture and helps cement Scott's place in the Liverpool hall of fame.

Ted Sagar played for Everton for an astonishing twenty-four years. He was so blue-blooded that the story did the rounds that his wife once said to him during an argument, 'Sometimes I think you love Everton more than you love me.' Ted supposedly replied, 'I even love Liverpool more than I love you.'

Anyway, if it hadn't been for the little matter that my asthma made me wheeze so much that my defenders thought Darth Vader was calling for the ball, I like to think I could have made the grade as a goalkeeper in the Bruce Grobbelaar mould. And I would never have let down my team. Not for all the char in China ... or all the zebras in Zimbabwe.

Mine was among the million hearts he broke on Merseyside when it emerged that he had apparently been intentionally con-ceding goals as part of betting scams, something he has continued to deny despite all the courtroom and taped evidence against him. I prefer to give the much maligned Grobbelaar the benefit of the doubt. I cannot believe he would stoop so low as to cheat on his team-mates and we fans ... and at his peak there have been few

Guess who's acting the clown. It's none other than Bruce Grobbelaar, who was a great entertainer at the back of the Liverpool defence. But it all ended with tears on the face of the clown.

goalkeepers to touch him. The picture I will fondly always carry of him in my memory is of when he was putting off the penalty takers with his 'spaghetti legs' antics in the 1984 European Cup final. Jerzy Dudek used the Grobb tactics but went even madder with the choreography during the unforgettable shoot-out against AC Milan in Istanbul in 2005. In future, perhaps goalkeepers should attend dancing classes!

The goalkeepers spotlighted in the following stories were not suspected of any dodgy business, but for a few moments at least there were doubts about their sanity.

Rio goalkeeper Isadore Irandir was deeply religious, and as his team prepared to face Corinthians in a Brazilian League match he went down on his knees on his goal line and offered a prayer for an injury-free match. He was still on his knees as Corinthians' world-renowned Roberto Rivelino collected the ball from the kick-off. He spotted Irandir in the praying position and struck the sweetest of shots Beckham-style from the halfway line high into the net. Time of goal? A then world-record five seconds.

It is not documented whether Irandir then prayed for forgiveness. Mike Bassett would have put his hands together – right around Irandir's throat. It was reported that a gun-wielding fan came running on to the pitch and fired three bullets into the ball as it nestled in the back of the net, which gave a whole new meaning to the phrase 'dead-ball situation'.

Manchester United centre-half Jackie Blanchflower went in goal as emergency stand-in for Ray Wood after the goalie had been carried off following a collision with Aston Villa's Peter McParland in the sixth minute of the 1957 FA Cup final. I heard Jackie say during an after-dinner speech that his main recollection of having to put on the goalkeeper's jersey was that 'it became the moment when I discovered that adrenalin is brown'.

Belfast bhoyo Jackie, older brother of that magnificent Tottenham and Northern Ireland skipper Danny Blanchflower, was a survivor of the Munich air crash that wiped out half the Manchester United team in 1958. He collected injuries that ended his career, but had the wit and the will to make a very good living as one of the funniest raconteurs on the after-dinner circuit. When Manchester United signed giant Danish international goalkeeper Peter Schmeichel Jackie held up to his audience the Manchester *Evening News* headline that read, 'United Sign Great Dane'. He said, 'For half that money I would have sold them my Dobermann. Now that would *really* have frightened the bejabers out of the opposition.'

On the opening day of the 2000–01 season Sheffield Wednesday goalkeeper Kevin Pressman carved himself a little niche in history by becoming the fastest red-carded player in the history of the Football League.

He was sent off playing against Wolves at Molineux for han-

dling the ball outside the box after just thirteen seconds! I've
heard of an early bath, but that's ridiculous.

In the early days of football goalkeepers could handle the ball anywhere
they liked, but the law was quickly changed after a game in which two
goalkeepers scored using their hands. Sounds like bloody netball.

I think somebody forgot to tell Ramon Quiroga that the rule had been
changed. He used to handle the ball yards out of the penalty area when
playing for Peru. Anybody who saw him booked for tackling a Polish
opponent in the 1978 World Cup finals will recall that he was several
sarnies short of a picnic. The tackle was made in the opponents' half of
the field!

As the ref – Englishman Pat Partridge – waved the yellow card,
Quiroga bowed in front of him like an actor taking the final-curtain
applause. He deserved an apple core rather than an encore.

Argentina needed five goals against Peru to qualify for the final
stages of that World Cup. I wonder if his Peruvian team-mates remembered that he had been born in, um, Argentina.

Confession time: I once let in ten goals in a match at Stanley Park,
so I know all about having to bend down to collect the ball after
it has gone past you. But my experience was nothing to that of
Nicky Salapu, goalkeeper for the Polynesian island of American
Samoa. He must have been suffering severe backache after retriev-
ing the ball from his net once every three minutes in a World Cup
qualifier against Australia in April 2001. The 31–0 scoreline is an
all-time World Cup record. I promise the following quote from the
Samoan manager is genuine: 'It would have been much worse if
our goalkeeper had not played brilliantly.'

The crowd played 'Spot the Goalkeeper' when East Stirlingshire took
on Albion Rovers on the last day of the 2002–03 Scottish League

season. East Stirlingshire's first goalkeeper went off injured early on, and his substitute was sent off. The third goalkeeper also got himself sent off, but goalie number four managed to save a penalty on the way to a 3–1 defeat. Jeepers keepers!

One of the best unintentional laughs I've ever been given by a goalkeeper was down to hundred-cap Bulgarian international Boris Mikhailov, who once played for Reading. He was as bald as the proverbial billiard ball, but astonished commentators during the 1994 World Cup finals by suddenly appearing with a full head of hair. Boris, bless him, had decided to use the exposure of the World Cup to promote a Bulgarian toupee company in which he had an interest (taking money off the top, so to speak).

It was just Boris's luck that the second-round match against Mexico was played in scorching, near-100-degree temperatures. The television cameras kept showing close-ups of poor Boris sweating buckets and continually adjusting the wig to try to cool his burning dome.

But he helped pull the rug from under the Mexicans and Bulgaria went through to the quarter-finals. Yes, Boris had a good hair day after all.

You must have seen the famous Scorpion save by shaggy-haired goal-keeper René Higuita when playing for Colombia against England at Wembley in 1995. He sprang forward on to the palms of his hands like a gymnast and kicked clear a Jamie Redknapp goal-bound effort with his feet high above his head. We discovered at that moment why his own manager called him 'El Loco'.

This was the same Higuita who, in the Italia '90 World Cup finals, cost Colombia the match against Cameroon by losing possession to Roger Milla when dribbling the ball ten yards outside his penalty area! And the same Higuita who was sent to jail for acting as a go-between with Colombia's notorious drug barons following a kidnapping. He was released after the charges against him were dropped. However, he had gone on a hunger strike and lost so much weight that he was not fit to join Colombia's 1994 World Cup squad. And the same Higuita who was suspended after failing a drugs test while playing in the Ecuadorian League in 2004. He was accused of taking cocaine. Perhaps he was too close to those drug barons. That's a fact not to be sniffed at.

Remarkably, Higuita scored more than twenty goals during his career. Yet even he has to take a back seat as a goalscoring goalkeeper to an incredible character called José Luis Chilavert, who played internationally for Paraguay and his club football in Argentina and Uruguay. He spent much of each match outside his area and was always hunting goals. His tally at the end of his career in 2003 was an unbelievable fifty-six goals, several of them scored in open play as well as from thumping free-kicks and penalties.

He once scored a hat-trick of penalties, and out-Becksed Beckham with a goal from just inside his own half. His goals were even more memorable because Chilavert invariably celebrated them by doing a tour of the pitch. He had a South American swagger to go with his skill, and said modestly at the close of his career, 'The greatest goalkeeper in the world is hanging up his gloves.' Pretentious, *moi*?

Chilavert's mantle as 'Mad King' was taken up by Belo Horizonte goalkeeper Fabiano. He was arrested by police and locked in the dressing-room after attacking a referee who had awarded a penalty against him. The game was held up for ten minutes while police wrestled with the raging Fabiano. When play resumed, with Fabiano safely shut away, his deputy saved the penalty.

Norwegian goalkeeper Olav Fiske was busting to relieve himself after a local cup tie had gone into extra-time. With a corner about to be taken at the other end, he decided he had time to do the business, and dashed to the touchline. He was just starting to water the grass when, to his horror, he saw the corner-kick cleared, and he was left holding his own as striker Oddvar Torve lobbed the ball into the unattended net from forty yards for a winning goal. His team-mates have not stopped taking the pee out of him since.

Sir Alex Ferguson has made some great buys during his golden reign at Old Trafford. Italian goalkeeper Massimo Taibi was not one of them. He cost a cool £4.5 million from Venezia as Sir Alex tried to replace the great Dane Peter Schmeichel. Taibi, who always seemed to be wearing tracksuit bottoms, made his debut against Liverpool and we got early evidence that he was, to say the least, a bit dodgy when he let in two soft goals. Then, playing against Southampton at Old Trafford, he let a mishit Matthew Le Tissier shot trickle through his legs. Eight days later he was 'missing in action' as Chelsea popped five goals into the United net.

Sir Alex had seen enough and moved Massimo out after little more than a month of mirth for all those not connected with United. They had a cracking nickname for him at Old Trafford – 'the Blind Venetian'.

That was an even better nickname than the one we hung on David James – 'Calamity James' – when he was suffering from dropsy at Anfield. On his day, James is as good as any goalkeeper in the world, but you always fear there's a howler waiting around the corner. He used to go on the catwalk as a male model, and the joke at Anfield was that he was like Stirling Moss on the catwalk and like Kate Moss in goal for us.

You had to have a streak of insanity to want to play in goal when I first started falling in love with the Beautiful Game. Those were the good old, mad old days when goalkeepers were fair game for centre-forwards, who had perfected the bruising art of using their shoulders as battering-rams. In today's softer, sanitised game goalies are protected by referees and rules to the point where a player risks an early bath if he as much as breathes on the goalkeeper. Consequently, goalies are not the great characters they used to be in an era when they risked grievous bodily harm every time they took the ball in their hands. They had to be strong and confident to survive, and bossed the penalty area with a mixture of bullying and bravado as they raced around, bouncing the ball with every step.

In tribute to these golden oldies of the goal line, let's go down memory lane for a while to remember some of the goalkeeping goliaths from the mists of myth and legend. I've already mentioned Mersey giants Ted Sagar and Elisha Scott, but even they were dwarfed by Albert Iremonger, one of the most astonishing characters ever to pull on the old green goalkeeper's jersey. (There was none of the floral-pattern gear as worn by today's namby-pambies, and gloves were more like mittens rather than the shovel-sized gloves they wear in the modern game.)

Albert played for the League's oldest club, Notts County, for twenty-one years from 1904. He became such a legendary figure that they named a Nottingham street after him. Iremonger used to think nothing of coming out of his penalty area to take throw-ins, free-kicks and even corner-kicks. 'The Long One' – six foot six tall and as lean as a lamppost – was always an excitable earthquake waiting to happen, and he used to have running arguments with referees. He once made such a nuisance of himself in a match at West Ham that a woman came on to the pitch and thumped him over the head with an umbrella. 'That'll teach you to get on with the game,' she yelled.

Albert always had an answer, no matter what the situation. He looked up to the sky and then said pleadingly to the woman, 'Let's borrow your umbrella, love. It looks like it's going to rain.'

When a referee was going to send off one of his team-mates for a brutal tackle, Albert ran from his goal line all the way to the opposite penalty area to implore, 'For goodness' sake, don't send *him* off, Ref. There'll be nothing left in our pockets when we get back to the dressing-room.'

In the days of *Chariots of Fire*, Albert followed a referee to the halfway line disputing a goal that had been awarded to Tottenham at White Hart Lane. The exasperated referee looked up into the face of the towering inferno that was Albert and said, 'Iremonger, I'm warning you just once. I'm sending you off if you're not back on your goal line in ten seconds.'

'Who d'you think I am?' replied our Albert. 'Harold blinking Abrahams?'

His favourite form of protest was to sit on the ball and refuse to return it after any debatable decision against him. He once clasped his long arms around Steve Bloomer after the Derby goalscorer had slipped the ball past him into the net.

'What are you up to, Albert?' said Bloomer.

'I'm kidnapping you,' said mad Albert. 'I'm holding you hostage until t'game's over. I'm not having you knocking any more goals past me.'

I hope you now have a mental picture of Albert because I'm coming up to one of my all-time favourite football stories, which has been passed down through generations of fans and is absolutely true.

Our Albert elected himself penalty-taker in a match against Sheffield Wednesday at Hillsborough. He took a twenty-yard run-up to the ball and hammered it with his considerable might. His shot hit the crossbar with such shuddering force that it rebounded past all the players as far as the halfway line.

There was a Keystone Kops-style chase back, led by the long-striding Albert. A Sheffield Wednesday player managed to help the ball on its way into the Notts County penalty area, and then a breathless Albert arrived on the scene just ahead of a mad scramble of players. He elected to kick the ball wide for a corner but instead managed to smash it into the back of his own net!

If Albert Iremonger was playing today he would be a national treasure.

Bill 'Fatty' Foulke was around at about the same time as Albert, and between them these two did more than anybody else to popularise the old football saying that 'all goalkeepers are crazy'.

Foulke was a mountain of a man, just over six foot two and weighing nearly twenty-three stones at his peak. For all his bulk, he was as light on his feet as a ballerina, and was sufficiently mobile to win an England cap and two FA Cup winners' medals with Sheffield United before becoming the toast of London town with Chelsea.

He could fist the ball almost as far as he could kick it, and it was his punching power that first earned him a place with a League club. A Sheffield United scout was watching him play for a Derbyshire colliery team when – attempting to punch the ball away – he missed and knocked out a rival forward's front teeth. When the scout explained what had happened, the Sheffield United manager replied, "'E'll do for me."

Big Bill was anything but a gentle giant. He had a volcanic temper, and once in a First Division game picked up a forward by his heels and hung him head-first above the ground, threatening to drop him, until he was persuaded by team-mates to let him down gently.

He once punched a hole in the dressing-room door in temper at a referee's decision, and threatened to do similar damage to Burslem referee Tom Kirkham after he had awarded a disputed goal against Sheffield United in the 1902 FA Cup final at Crystal Palace. Foulke came out of the United dressing-room stark naked and chased Kirkham along the corridor. The referee had the good sense to lock himself in his room until the raging bull had been calmed down. 'I have never seen a sight quite like it,' said Mr Kirkham. A goalkeeper with bouncing balls. So what's new?

When he was invited to a Sheffield theatre during a United Cup run the management had to make three seats into one for him. They laid on a spread before the show and Big Bill was the first to arrive. He had demolished most of the food meant for the entire team before any of his team-mates showed up. He was quite happy to answer to the pre-PC nickname of Fatty, which was fortunate, because by the time he was winding down his career with Chelsea his weight had gone up past twenty-five stones. He quickly became a hero at Stamford Bridge with his eccentric behaviour, preferring to kick the ball off the line because he could not get down to save it.

Sadly, in a book designed to make you smile, I have to introduce a depressing note. Big Bill, who earned peanuts during his career, hit tough times after hanging up his gloves and had to suffer the humiliation of working as a sideshow attraction in Blackpool. 'Penny a shot, twopence back if you score against the famous Fatty Foulke,' was the showmaster's cry. Poor old, under-fed Bill caught pneumonia standing out in the rain fielding penalties for his bread and butter, and he died at the age of forty. But he lives on as a legendary figure in football: Bill Foulke, the football folk-hero.

When I was a kid growing up in Liverpool and starting a lifelong love affair with football, the greatest goalkeeper around was England regular Frank Swift. Like Albert Iremonger and Fatty Foulke before him, he was larger than life, and deliberately turned himself into a showman because he believed that spectators deserved entertainment for their entrance money.

Swiftie, who famously fainted on his goal line at the final whistle after helping Manchester City win the 1934 FA Cup final, would pick up opponents in his huge hands if they dared to charge him, go down on one knee and pretend to shoot them as they approached with the ball at their feet, and he would often kneel, pleading, in front of referees when decisions went against him.

My favourite Swiftie story is one that he told himself at his testimonial dinner, not long before he was tragically killed in the 1958 Munich air crash while travelling with the Busby Babes as a *News of the World* reporter. He took only one penalty in his marvellous career with Man City, and this is how he recalled it:

We were winning a wartime match 5–0 when the skipper invited me to take a spot-kick. A team-mate placed the ball on the spot and I started my run-up from the edge of my own penalty area. I hit the ball with all my might and it smashed into the goal with such force that it ripped a hole in the net and carried on through. The ball banged into the face of an old boy standing on the terraces behind the goal and when I went to apologise he showed me that I had broken his false teeth. I never again had the appetite to take another penalty.

And, presumably, the old boy had no appetite to eat without his false teeth.

The late, great Sam Bartram could lay some claim to being football's first sweeper. He continually used to come out of his penalty area when playing in goal for Charlton Athletic in the immediate post-war years, dribbling the ball clear before passing to a team-mate.

Sam, who used to stand out with his flaming red hair, had a story to tell that went well with that blaze on his head:

We were playing in an away cup match on one of those cramped non-League grounds where you could almost feel the breath of the spectators on your back. The referee made an unpopular decision that infuriated the home fans, who started bombarding me with orange peel and coins.

Unbeknown to me, somebody had also thrown a lighted cigarette-end, which somehow got caught in the goal netting and set it on fire. The first I knew of it was when our trainer came dashing from the touchline and threw his bucket of water on to the flames. After we had won the tie, the opposition centre-forward said, 'At least we've gone out in a blaze of glory.'

Jack Fairbrother, Newcastle United's goalkeeper when they won the FA Cup in 1951, once mislaid his gloves before a game and borrowed a pair from a friendly policeman. Newcastle won the match, and from then on Jack always insisted on wearing policemen's white gloves. It is not true that every time he saved the ball, he shouted, 'You've been nicked.'

Pat Jennings, arguably the greatest goalkeeper of them all with Tottenham, Arsenal and Northern Ireland, scored one of the most astonishing goals ever seen at Old Trafford during the 1967 curtain-raising Charity Shield match.

Pat was the second most surprised man in the ground when his drop-kick from the Tottenham penalty area went first bounce into the back of the Manchester United net. Even more astonished was United goalkeeper Alex Stepney, who had been an interested spectator on the edge of the United penalty area when the ball suddenly sailed over his head.

Jennings said later, 'It was a once-in-a-lifetime goal. I could never have done it without the wind behind me. The funniest thing was seeing my Tottenham team-mates looking at each other in utter bewilderment, wondering who to congratulate for the goal. Most of them didn't know where the ball had come from because they had their backs to me when I took the kick. Jimmy Greaves said to Alan Gilzean, "D'you realise that this makes Pat our top scorer!"'

A pat on the back for Pat.

Playing for Colchester, goalkeeper Graham Smith went through his usual pre-match ritual of kicking the foot of each of his posts. He kicked one post, jogged across the goal line, and kicked the other. Then the crossbar fell on his head.

One of the greatest character goalkeepers to play for Liverpool was Tommy Lawrence, a Scot we affectionately nicknamed 'the Flying Pig'. He was a hefty guy who used to throw himself around like a demented gymnast. A story that has gathered strength over the years is that during one of the derby games at Goodison the score was 0–0 with a minute to go. One of the Everton players broke clear and scuffed a hopeful shot that trickled through Tommy's legs and into the net for the winning goal.

Manager Bill Shankly, his face redder than a Liverpool shirt, was waiting for Tommy as he walked into the dressing-room.

'Sorry, Boss,' said a downcast Lawrence. 'I should have kept my legs closed.'

'Oh no,' spat Shanks. 'It wasnae you who should have kept your legs closed. It was your mother!'

Port Vale's defenders couldn't understand why their goalkeeper was scrambling around on his hands and knees in the goalmouth after Sheffield United had scored an early goal in a Second Division match in 1892. Legend has it that one defender went to enquire what was wrong when there was the sound of breaking glass. He had trodden on the spectacles for which the goalkeeper had been searching. Port Vale went on to lose 0–10. It remains the heaviest home defeat in League football, and the goalkeeper made a right spectacle of himself.

Dave Beasant had quite a day at Wembley on 14 May 1988. I remember it well because Liverpool were on the receiving end of his charmed performance. Playing for 'no hopers' Wimbledon, he became the first goalkeeper to save a penalty in an FA Cup final. What made it all the more remarkable was that it was against John 'Deadeye' Aldridge, who had successfully put away eleven penalties for Liverpool that season.

Then Dave became the first goalkeeper to collect the FA Cup as a winning captain, and he was also the first to do it wearing one glove. 'I only had time to pull off one of my gloves to shake hands with the VIPs,' he said later.

Funny how fate in football can either elevate you to moments beyond your dreams or suddenly kick you in the balls. A couple of years later, after he had moved to Chelsea, Dave dropped a bottle of salad cream on his foot, severed a tendon and put himself not only out of action for two months but out of the running for any more England caps.

But he prefers to remember Wimbledon's 'Cinderella' run to the FA Cup in 1988. They were his salad days.

Scottish international goalkeeper Andy Goram was described in a Glasgow newspaper as 'being a bit of a schizophrenic'. The following weekend, when he was playing for Rangers against Kilmarnock, the fans started chanting, 'Two Andy Gorams, there's only two Andy Gorams . . .'

It was a dog-day afternoon for goalkeeper Chic Brodie when he was playing for Brentford in a match against Colchester in 1970. A black-and-white terrier came racing on to the pitch, upended a linesman and then chased a back pass meant for Brodie. Everybody thought it was hilarious when he went down to collect the ball and got an armful of mad dog instead. But it was not funny for Chic, who was so badly injured as the terrier collided with him that he was carried off and never played top-flight football again. It was all captured by the television cameras, and has gone down in sporting legend as the day football went barking mad.

Reflecting on his career some years later, Chic described himself as a one-man disaster area. 'As well as the dog incident,' he said, 'the goal once collapsed on me at Lincoln, I had a hand grenade thrown at me when playing against Millwall, and I was the most injury- and accident-prone person ever.'

But even Chic could not match the injuries that sidelined the following goalkeepers:

Alex Stepney dislocated his jaw shouting at his Man United defenders . . . David Seaman pulled a muscle reaching for the TV

Goalkeeping can put years on you, but this is ridiculous! Peterborough goalie Fred Barber used to come out on to the pitch wearing an old man's mask. He said he just wanted to give the fans a laugh. Let's face it, he succeeded.

Copyright © popperfoto.com

remote-control . . . Andy Dibble was taken to hospital suffering from chemical burns after diving on a pitch that had been treated with fertiliser . . . Chris Woods sliced his finger with a penknife while trying to free himself from his jammed tracksuit bottoms . . . Kasey Keller knocked out his front teeth while pulling his golf bag from the boot of his car . . . Liverpool reserve goalie Michael Stensgaard dislocated his shoulder erecting an ironing board . . . Jim Leighton had to leave the pitch after losing a contact lens . . . Wycombe's Australian 'keeper Frank Talia sliced off a toe when he managed to fall over while mowing his lawn . . . And, topping them all, one goalkeeper put himself out of action on a match day when getting his head caught in his car door. I will protect his identity, otherwise people will be laughing their heads off at him.

I am ducking outside the League for one of my favourite goalkeeping stories, which involves a player who, for reasons that will become obvious, must remain anonymous.

He took a mobile phone on to the pitch with him while playing in a match in the Medway Sunday League in Kent in 1999. Just as the game was about to kick off he took a call, and then refused the referee's orders to hang up. Our goalkeeping hero paused in his telephone chat just long enough to give the referee his name before continuing his chat. The referee reported him to the League, and it turned out that he had given a false name and was not registered with his club. Asked why he chose goalkeeper as his position, he said he had a calling.

I make that alleged joke as a link to another goalkeeper, who fits perfectly into the crazy category. He was a young goalie with Coventry City and Hereford before knee problems forced him into premature retirement, and he launched a career as a sports presenter with the BBC. His name, of course, was David Icke, who later became rather better known as the self-described Son of God, preaching to all and sundry while wearing garish turquoise shell-suits.

As well as predicting that Jesus was shortly coming back to save the world, Icke warned that Cuba, the White Cliffs of Dover and the Isle of Aran would be disappearing, and that the Channel Tunnel would never be built – this despite the foundation-laying that was going on at the time.

If I'd had the chance, I wanted to ask him one question: why did he allow Maradona to use his dad's hand to score against England in the 1986 World Cup finals?

You've gotta laugh

Shortly after signing Spanish international Fernando Hierro, Bolton manager Sam Allardyce called a team meeting. He began by drawing a diagram of a ball and a goal on a blackboard, speaking very, very slowly and carefully articulating every word.

'This is a ball,' he said. 'And this is a goal net.'

'You can talk normally, Boss,' piped up Wanderers midfielder Gary Speed. 'Fernando speaks perfect English.'

'I'm not talking to Fernando,' Allardyce replied. 'This is for the rest of you!'

A League footballer – he played for United – got blind drunk with team-mates after a defeat, and when he staggered home at three o'clock the morning after the match he found his wife had locked him out. Even in his drunken state he knew he was better off not trying to get into the house because she would have killed him, so he walked the mile to his club's training ground. As he was clambering into the dressing-room through the unlocked window he fell in head-first. The window blew shut and it shattered, sending splinters of glass into his arse. When he took off his trousers, ready to sleep on the treatment table, he looked at the full-length mirror and saw blood dripping from deep gashes on his buttocks. He was still drunk out of his head, but realised that he needed to do something to stop the bleeding. He went to the medical cupboard, took out a tin of plasters and, using the mirror to guide him, covered the cuts.

The next morning he woke up with a blinding hangover and an aching arse. He slowly realised where he was, and then got back out of the window before the manager could find out where he'd spent the night. In the local paper later that week, a story read: 'Vandals broke into the United training ground this week, smashed a window in the dressing-room and stuck plasters all over the full-length mirror.'

Hark who's talking

Kevin Keegan:
'Goalkeepers aren't born today until they're in their late twenties or thirties.'

Neville Southall:
'If you don't believe you can win, there's no point in getting out of bed at the end of the day.'

Jim Platt:
'I cannot see us getting beaten once we get our tails in front.'

George Graham:
'The goalkeeper is the jewel in the crown and getting at him should be almost impossible. It's the biggest sin in football to make him do any work.'

Malcolm Allison:
'Our 'keeper Joe Corrigan may be concussed, but it's difficult to tell with him because he always looks a bit dopey.'

Andy Gray:
'Liverpool goalkeeper Chris Kirkland's future is definitely in front of him.'

Bruce Grobbelaar:
'That's a question mark everybody's asking.'

Frank Swift:
'When I see Tommy Lawton going up for the ball I wonder if he's got a parachute on his back. He comes down from enormous heights.'

Peter Bonetti:
'It's vital that a goalkeeper makes himself heard and should shout as loud as possible, "My balls" when crosses come over.'

Sam Bartram:
'Stanley Matthews was so mesmerising that all he had to do was dip a shoulder and our defenders

would tackle thin air and I would dive for a ball that wasn't there. It was like trying to play against a hypnotist.'

Pat Jennings:
'Jimmy Greaves was the greatest one-on-one finisher ever. If it was between him and the 'keeper Jimmy would win every time. He was on my side and I could never tell which way he was going to go with the ball. I wonder how good he would have been if he'd trained properly. He was the one who used to get lifts on the milk float during pre-season cross-country runs!'

Peter Schmeichel:
'What we have to do is put our teeth into the Premiership.'

Harry Gregg:
'Nat Lofthouse used to knock ten skittles of excrement out of you, and then after the match buy you a beer.

He was a lovely bloke until he put on the number-nine shirt. Then he would become Rocky Marciano in football boots.'

Gil Merrick:
'I can honestly say that the thirteen goals the Hungarians put past me in two matches would have been scored regardless of who was between the posts. They were footballers from another planet.'

Shaka Hislop:
'It was like déjà vu all over again.'

Dave Beasant:
'If you make the right decision, it's normally going to be the correct one.'

Ian Walker:
'Maybe the mistakes have looked worse because they led to goals!'

5 Managing to Laugh

My alter ego Mike Bassett knows only too well that managing a football team is the most demanding job in sport, on a par with trying to keep the *Titanic* afloat while carrying the weight of expectation of thousands of supporters, and at the mercy of posturing, overpaid players and the daggers from backstabbing directors. The best description I ever heard of a manager came from the old warhorse Joe Mercer, who said during his peak years in harness with Malcolm Allison at Manchester City: 'You need the skin of a rhinoceros, the motivating powers of an evangelist, the luck of a pools winner, and the balance of a tightrope walker, because you are just one step from a fall, and there's no safety-net.'

One other thing managers need is a good sense of humour. Ulcers can be kept at bay if managers learn to laugh even when things are going wrong, and, as you will read in this chapter, there are many of them who, um, manage to laugh.

I've had my fair share of managing experience in the real football world at grassroots level. When my asthma got so bad I had to hang up my playing boots, I managed several pub teams and was a master at giving the bucket-and-cold-sponge treatment. I once ran on to treat a player who had been kicked right in the goolies, and I got the sponge to work on the damaged territory. 'Don't rub them,' he said. 'Count them.' OK, not original, but true.

An ITV show gave an alarming picture of the stresses and strains on football managers. The programme-makers monitored the hearts of two Premiership bosses – Bolton's Sam Allardyce, and Dave (no relation to Mike) Bassett, who was then in the Leicester hot seat. The monitors were checked as their teams battled through a 2–2 draw. The results were frightening – almost heart-stopping. Allardyce's rate went from 46 per minute to 160 when the action was at its most frenzied, while Bassett's heart muscles contracted ominously when his midfield player Muzzy Izzet was sent off. Health experts were called in to analyse the results, and they said what the two managers had gone through was the equivalent of what soldiers face in the heat of battle.

But it's not only the managers who suffer. England Under-21 boss Peter Taylor tells a moving story that illustrates what the pressures of management can do to those near and dear. Shortly after he had been ruthlessly sacked by Leicester City in the opening weeks of the 2001–02 season, he received a telephone call from his twenty-one-year-old daughter, who was holidaying in Ibiza.

'I was hypnotised on stage last night, Dad,' she told him. 'Apparently the hypnotist asked me what I would do if I won a million pounds, and I said I would bomb Leicester.'

Proof positive of how the stress is carried by a manager's family and friends. Only a game? Don't make me laugh.

Bertie Mee, the manager who led Arsenal to the League and FA Cup double in 1970–71, said, 'Managing is an eight-days-a-week job. You have to eat it and sleep it. My children see so little of me that they call me "The man who eats cornflakes with us".'

I loved the approach to management of that old fox Alec Stock. He used to hang a notice in the dressing-room that read: 'When we train, we train as well as we can. When we play, we play as well as we can. And when we stop and have a beer, we will be bloody good at that, too.'

With that as the philosophy, let's now get on with my favourite anecdotes about managers in the mad, mad, mad world of football.

Some exceptional scriptwriters put the words into the mouth of Mike Bassett, but even they could not match this true cracker in the heat of battle from Scottish manager John Lambie. During a Partick Thistle match, the trainer ran on to treat the centre-forward after he had been knocked out in a collision with the goalkeeper.

'He's got concussion,' the trainer reported.

'Great,' responded Lambie. 'Tell him he's Pele and send him back on.'

John Beck gained notoriety as one of the most eccentric of all managers. Just to give you an idea of his reputation, Radio 5 Live greeted the news of his reappointment as Cambridge United manager with the chilling line, 'Just when you thought it was safe to go back into the showers . . .' They accompanied this with the music from Hitchcock's *Psycho*.

The reference they were making was to the famed (and feared) cold showers that he instructed the Cambridge players to take before a game. This was the same John Beck who had a half-time fist-fight with his top striker Steve Claridge during a dispute over playing tactics. And the same John Beck whose gamesmanship tricks included overheating the opposition dressing-room, soaking their practice balls for the pre-match warm-up in water, ordering the grass to be kept long in the corners of the Cambridge pitch, sanding the goal areas to suit his team's tactics, and – it was alleged – ordering tea for the visiting players to be laced with salt.

Notorious for his long balls ('Now there's a novelty,' I can hear Eric Morecambe saying), Beck had a sense of humour to go with his eccentricity. He once said, 'I have been nicknamed Dracula because I am accused of sucking the life out of football.'

This story, told by the doyen of football managers Sir Bobby Robson, shows that the competitive edge that exists these days between Alex Ferguson and Arsène Wenger has always been part and parcel of football management:

We [Ipswich] had battled to a draw in the FA Cup against Cloughie's Nottingham Forest in the early eighties. I wanted to suggest to Brian that we switch the replay from a Tuesday to a Wednesday because of a fixture pile-up.

I politely tapped on Cloughie's office door and went in. He was sitting at his desk with his skipper Larry Lloyd and his assistant Ronnie Fenton either side of him.

'What the f*** do you want?' Cloughie asked sharply.

I explained about the possibility of switching the match, and all he said was 'F*** off, you.'

That was it. He had nothing more to say. He had taught me a lesson that managers have to learn the hard way: never give a manager an even break.

Cloughie, of course, was a one-off. I remember the inimitable Bill Shankly once saying, 'Whenever I talk to that man I am never sure whether he is drunk with alcohol or arrogance.'

His tactical talk before one major match was to hold up the ball so that all his players could see it, and then said. 'This is a football. Go out there and play with it as though you own it.'

With that, he walked out of the dressing-room.

Millions saw the barmy side of Brian when the Tottenham–Forest FA Cup final went into extra-time in 1991. Bizarrely, while Spurs manager Terry Venables was out on the pitch coaxing and encouraging his players in the short break, Cloughie passed the time of day with a policeman. Spurs went on to win 2–1 when Forest defender Des Walker deflected the ball into his own net. The FA Cup was the one trophy that always eluded Cloughie, who said of the policeman incident:

'He was a very nice chap and I was interested in what sort of day he was having. Trying to crowd thoughts into players' minds at that stage is pretty pointless. If they don't know what to do by then they should not be professional footballers.'

There will never be another quite like Brian Clough.

Cloughie admitted being heavily influenced in his approach to management by a boss out of the old school – Harry Storer, an outstanding all-round sportsman who managed at Coventry, Birmingham and Derby after playing for England as a half-back and scoring seventeen centuries as a hard-hitting Derbyshire batsman.

Harry was a tough, uncompromising character who could never forgive any player putting in anything less than 100 per cent on the pitch. When scouting for Everton late in his career, he submitted his report on a player with just one word scrawled on the page in capital letters: 'COWARD'.

This was Joe Mercer's favourite Harry Storer tale:

In my early days as a manager at Sheffield United we played Harry's Derby County who, to say the least, put the boot about a bit. I saw Harry immediately after the game and said, 'I don't know why you bothered to put a ball out on the pitch. Two of your players didn't need one. They kicked us instead.'

'Oh,' said Harry, 'which two were they? I want their names.'

I was a bit embarrassed. 'Well, I don't want to get them into trouble,' I mumbled.

'They're not the ones in trouble,' said Harry, with deadly seriousness. 'It's the other nine I'm after!'

Harry Storer anecdotes are thick on the ground. He once took a Derby player out on to the pitch on a Monday morning and got on all fours in the penalty area as if looking for something he had lost.

'What you looking for, Boss?' asked the startled player.

'The bloody hole you were hiding in on Saturday,' yelled Harry.

Vic Buckingham was another eccentric boss, at West Brom, Fulham and Barcelona, the club he gloriously led to the Spanish title. He had the young, gifted Rodney Marsh in his Fulham squad, and once took him on to an empty pitch and started jiving and dancing around, while singing the George Gershwin classic 'I've Got Rhythm'. Rodney looked on open-mouthed. 'This is what football's all about, son,' said Vic. 'It's called rhythm.'

Buckingham came in for a bucketful of criticism from Fulham fans when he sold crowd-pleaser Rodney to near-neighbours Queen's Park Rangers. He told pressmen privately, 'If I had wanted a clown, I would have signed Coco.'

Arsène Wenger, the extraordinarily successful Arsenal manager, is nicknamed 'Clouseau' by the few English players at Highbury. Ray Parlour recalled that before one game Wenger ushered his players into the tunnel before excusing himself to go to the toilet. While he was doing his business there was a security alert and the players were told to return to the dressing-room. Wenger did a double take when he emerged from the toilet to find his squad milling around him. He asked in his heavy French accent, 'What is up? Why are you back here?'

Parlour, in a spot-on Peter Sellers impersonation, said, 'There is a *burm*.'

Wenger replied, classically, 'A *burm*?'

As everyone fell about laughing, Parlour continued with the routine: 'Yes, a *burm*.'

When the laughter had stopped, Wenger said, 'Raymond . . . I do believe you are having a joke with me.'

Football my Arsène!

I love the stories of managers who throw and kick things in the dressing-room, and I would have given Mike Bassett's salary to have been a fly on the wall when Sir Alex Ferguson and David Beckham had their flying-boot altercation. A boot kicked in anger by Fergie, after a Man United defeat by Arsenal, landed above Beckham's eye. He had to have stitches inserted, and Posh was said to be so livid she wanted her man to strangle Fergie with his sarong. It's not true that Becks had said, 'On me 'ead, son.'

Even better was the incident after another Man United–Arsenal match at Old Trafford when a pizza, allegedly thrown by Gunners left-back Ashley Cole, missed intended target Ruud van Nistelrooy and splattered Alex Ferguson instead.

But most dramatic of all the food-chucking sagas was when Grimsby manager Brian Laws hurled a plate of chicken sandwiches across the dressing-room at Italian striker Ivano Bonetti after a 3–2 defeat. What could have been funny turned deadly serious. The plate whacked Bonetti in the face and fractured his cheekbone, and the legal eagles were summoned.

The Italian shouted, 'Fowl!'

You can't keep that man Cloughie out of any collection of dressing-room bust-ups. He admitted taking it out with his fists on the likes of Roy Keane, Nigel Jemson and, brave man, Stuart 'Psycho' Pearce. But best of all from Cloughie was when he whacked fans who had invaded the pitch in full view of the television cameras.

Cloughie was unrepentant. 'You have my permission', he joked, 'to say the shit hit the fan.'

Trevor Francis seemed to have been strongly influenced by his old boss Cloughie when managing Crystal Palace. He was so incensed when he spotted substitute goalkeeper Alex Kolinko laughing after Palace had conceded a soft goal against Bradford that he clouted him around the head. The FA fined Francis a thousand pounds, which was not fine with him.

Lawrie McMenemy, who enjoyed heady days at Southampton, was involved in one of the most spectacular dressing-room punch-ups. He had a barney with England central defender Mark Wright after a Saints defeat in 1984, and they eventually had to be pulled apart as their disagreement degenerated into a wrestling match in the showers.

It was headlined 'The Saint versus the Sinner'.

Ever wondered why on Merseyside they shout, 'Taxi!' whenever a manager is struggling? It goes back to 1961 when Johnny Carey, a legend as a player with Man United, was manager of Everton, then in fifth place in the old First Division. Carey shared a cab ride with his chairman John Moores after a League clubs conference in London. As the taxi crawled through the capital's rush-hour traffic the chairman, the millionaire owner of Littlewoods, took the opportunity to tell his manager that the board had decided to sack him. 'I saw to it that Mr Moores paid the fare,' said Carey. *Taxi!*

Managers have to learn to laugh with their players if they're going to win their respect. Keith Burkinshaw, for example, had to laugh after almost literally putting his foot in it while boss at Tottenham.

Spurs were on a club tour of Japan, and had a courtesy visit arranged to the British embassy in Tokyo. Terry Naylor, one of the jokers in the Tottenham pack, convinced Burkinshaw that the custom was for everybody visiting the ambassador to remove their shoes and socks as a mark of respect before entering the main reception room.

Once he had got Keith hooked, Terry primed the rest of the squad. When they got to the embassy, they all went through the motions of untying their shoelaces. Then Burkinshaw led the party into the ambassador's reception room and, of course, was the only bare-footed person in the building. I bet he felt a right burk.

Stan Cullis, the master of Molineux, was one of the strictest managers ever, and ran a tight, disciplined ship during his outstanding reign as manager of Wolves in the days when they ruled the football world. He was once tearing into his players following a poor performance when he noticed out of the corner of his eye that one of the reserves was smiling. 'I don't know what you've got to laugh about,' he roared. 'You're not even good enough to get into the team.'

Scot Symon, one of the most successful Glasgow Rangers managers, was infamous for his insistence on not talking to the press. He preferred his teams to do their talking on the pitch.

A journalist once telephoned him at Ibrox on the day of a scheduled midweek match in the 1960s. 'If this fog doesn't lift there's not much chance of the game being played this evening, is there?' the reporter asked in a friendly tone.

'I never comment on the weather,' snapped Symon and slammed down the receiver.

Gordon Strachan has always got a witty comeback, and I thought it was football's loss when he took a break from managing while doing a very good job with Southampton. When Ecuadorian forward Agustin Delgado was on trial with the Saints he played in a reserve match, and Strachan said of his performance: 'You can't read too much into that game because Agustin was virtually up against their youth team. I've never seen so much acne on a football pitch.' They could have played spot the ball.

Former Newcastle manager and club captain Joe Harvey was a fanatical gardener. One night he came home to find a burglar in his house. Joe chased the intruder out of the back door, and as he pursued him across the garden shouted, 'Whatever you do, don't tread on my roses.'

When he gave a player a trial after a strong recommendation from the club scout, Harvey wrote dismissively on his report card: 'Can't trap a medicine ball.'

Sir Bobby Robson was often good for a laugh while manager of England – but not always intentionally. After England had scraped past Cameroon in the 1990 World Cup finals he said, 'We didn't underestimate them. They were better than we thought.'

Goalkeeper Peter Shilton played his last match for England in the third-place play-off in the 1990 finals, which was also Bobby's final game in charge. Paying tribute to Shilts, his manager said, 'What can I say about Peter Shilton? Peter Shilton is Peter Shilton and he has been Peter Shilton since the year dot.'

The tabloids had muck-raking fun at Robson's expense by claiming that he was having extracurricular get-togethers with not one but two redheads – not at the same time, I hasten to add. Could this explain why he fancied Alan Ball and Paul Scholes as players?

During his days as manager of West Bromwich Albion, Ron Atkinson was close friends with the then Birmingham City boss Jim Smith. One evening they went together to see comedian Billy Connolly, who was appearing at the Birmingham Hippodrome. After the show they were invited into the Big Yin's dressing-room. Smithy asked Billy if he found it easy to communicate with Midlands audiences.

'Och aye,' said Billy. 'I love playing Birmingham.'

'Don't we all,' said Atko. 'Don't we all.'

When he moved from West Brom to manage Man United, Atko inherited a team that included Ray Wilkins. It was Atkinson who nicknamed him 'The Crab', 'because he only moves sideways'.

In his first season at Old Trafford, Lancashire Cricket Club borrowed the ground for a floodlit cricket match. As the groundsmen were marking out the wicket in the middle of the pitch, Atko summoned Wilkins to join him on the touchline.

'Look, Ray,' he said, pointing, 'they're marking out your territory.'

Ray was stumped for an answer.

I could have filled this book with quotes I have collected from managers over the years. For your amusement, I have decided to concentrate on three of the most charismatic, controversial and captivating managers of my time looking in from the outside on the Beautiful Game.

First is the manager who was my personal favourite – the one and only Bill Shankly, the swaggering, self-assured Scot who lit the flame of the red revolution at Liverpool that burns brightly to this day.

Like so many of the truly outstanding managers, he could rarely find a gracious thing to say for any team that beat his side. Following a 5–1 embarrassment in Europe against Ajax – including a barnstorming performance from a then unknown youngster called Johan Cruyff – Shanks growled, 'Och, we just got frustrated against their defensive tactics.'

Shanks was one of the first of the spin-doctor managers, who could turn facts on their head to boost the confidence of his players. During a team talk before a match against Manchester United, for example, he once knocked the Subbuteo players representing George Best, Denis Law and Bobby Charlton off the tactical table and said in that distinctive voice of his, 'Don't worry about them – they cannae play the game. Let's talk about *our* team.'

Liverpool legends Bob Paisley and Bill Shankly managed to do everything brilliantly – except spell 'goal' correctly! I was lucky to get to know both of them, and what they had in common – as well as unsurpassed tactical knowledge – was blood that flowed Liverpool red. We won't see their like again.

He once went to the loo to relieve himself during a sporting-club dinner in Manchester. He was going about his business when the bloke standing next to him suddenly realised who he was, um, rubbing shoulders with. He did a double-take and spun around, saying, 'Hey, you're Bill Shankly.'

'Aye,' said a purple-faced Shanks. 'And you're pissing all down my trousers.'

At another dinner, Shanks was being lauded by a speaker who told the audience, 'Bill will always be remembered as a great manager, but let us not forget that he was also a great player. Many of you here will be too young to have seen him in action, but I can tell you that he was the finest half-back Preston ever had.' From the top table came the shout, 'Aye, he's right, ye know.' Shanks was doing the seconding.

Phil Thompson was so skinny when he joined Liverpool as a young lad from school that Shanks ordered, 'Put him on a steak diet. I've seen more flesh on a sparrow.' A year or so later Phil told Shanks that he was planning to get married. 'Married?' boomed Shanks. 'My God, we've bred a monster.'

Shankly hated holidays abroad because there was nobody with whom he could talk football apart from his long-suffering, lovely wife Nessie. He came back from one overseas trip admitting it had been better than he had expected. 'We got up a team in the hotel and beat the waiters,' he said.

For years it was rumoured that Shankly had taken Nessie on a visit to watch Rochdale reserves on their wedding anniversary. Finally, he issued a denial, saying with a poker face, 'As if I would have got married in the football season. It was Nessie's birthday.'

Always conscious of the great rivalry with Everton, Shanks once said, 'There are two great sides on Merseyside: Liverpool and Liverpool reserves.'

Asked by the barber if he would like 'anything off the top' in the Goodison championship season of 1969–70, he said, 'Aye, Everton.'

The Liverpool team were staying near Lake Como on the eve of a European Cup semi-final against Inter Milan. The players had just gone to bed when a bell started ringing in a nearby monastery. Shanks, convinced it was a plot to keep them awake, picked up his bedside telephone and rang the interpreter, who was staying in the same hotel.

'What's that ringing?' Shanks demanded.

'It's the monastery bell, Mr Shankly,' explained the bewildered interpreter.

'Well, ring the head monk and tell him I want it stopped this minute,' snapped Shanks, slamming down the receiver.

The interpreter called back a few minutes later and said, 'I'm sorry, Mr Shankly, but the bell-ringing has some holy significance and I cannot get it stopped.'

Shanks thought for a moment, and then said, 'Ring the head monk back and tell him to put a bloody bandage around his damned bell.'

There have been few better-behaved footballers – on and off the pitch – than Ian Callaghan. He was a marvellous ambassador for the game in general and for Liverpool Football Club in particular. There was just one occasion when Ian broke his good-conduct code. He had a drink or three too many during a club trip to Belgium and, along with a group of Liverpool team-mates, broke a curfew. Shanks was waiting for them when they returned to the hotel in the early hours. He gave each of the players a bollocking, and then turned to face Callaghan, who was just about legless. 'And you, Ian Callaghan . . . you of all people,' Shanks said in a fury, obviously searching for the right words. 'You . . . I'm going to tell your wife on you.'

A reporter likened the Sheffield United schemer Tony Currie to Tom Finney in Shankly's hearing. 'Aye, you're right,' he said. 'He is very nearly in Tom's class, but let's remember that Tom is now nearly sixty.' He then added: 'Tom Finney could play in an overcoat and beat any defender around today.'

England international left-back Bob McNab was being shown around Anfield by Shanks, who had agreed terms for his transfer from Huddersfield. 'You'll be joining the greatest club in the world, son,' Shanks said, with his usual gift for understatement. 'We've got the best players, the best fans, the best facilities. You're a quality player and this is the right club for you.'

After all his sales talk, Shanks was surprised to hear McNab say that he wanted time to think things over. Two days later, Bob telephoned Shanks from Highbury to tell him that he had decided to sign for Arsenal. 'Och,' said Shanks. 'They're welcome to you. You never could play the game anyway. I only wanted you for our reserves.'

Shanks was less than happy when a match at Orient was called off because of a waterlogged pitch. He sorted out the groundsman and told him, 'The trouble with this ground is that you've got just ordinary grass. Come up to Anfield and see our pitch. We've got *professional* grass.'

Booking into a hotel in the United States, he put alongside 'home address' on the registration form: 'Anfield'.

Once after an FA Cup final at Wembley two Liverpool fans bent down and kissed Shanks' feet. 'While you're down there, lads,' their hero said, 'gi'e my shoes a polish.'

Told by a referee that a player had not been offside because he was not interfering with play, Shanks responded, 'If he's not interfering with play, what the bloody hell is he doing on the pitch?'

Shanks used to take part in the training matches while manager, and played every game as competitively as if it were a cup final. Chris Lawler, new to the club and very shy and uncommunicative, was standing watching a five-a-side match when Bill insisted he had scored before the ball had been kicked off the line.

'Chris, son,' he said, 'you saw that. Was that shot of mine over the line?'

Honest Chris said, 'No, Boss. It was cleared.'

Bill put his hands on his hips and gave his best James Cagney pose. 'That's the first words ye've spoken since ye've been here and it's a lie,' said Shanks.

Ian St John says that he was once discussing tactics with Shanks, who told him, 'If you're not sure what to do with the ball, just pop it in the net and we'll discuss your options afterwards.'

Following a contract dispute with Anfield iron man Tommy Smith, Shanks said, 'He could start a riot in a graveyard.'

Introducing giant new signing Ron Yeats, he told the press, 'He's a colossus. Come and walk round him and inspect him for yourself.'

Yeats eventually became captain, and after a defeat in a match Shanks asked him what he had called when he tossed the coin before the kick-off.

'Heads,' said Yeats.

'Och,' said Shanks, with a shake of his head. 'You should have called tails.'

A posse of Italian journalists were shouting questions at Shanks after a controversial match in Milan. He watched the interpreter fielding the questions and then said, 'Tell them that whatever they're saying, I disagree with them.'

For the return leg with Milan, he guarded his team plans as if they were state secrets. He said, 'I'm not giving away any information to Milan. If I had my way, I wouldn't even tell them the time of the kick-off.'

Finally, perhaps his most famous quote of all: 'Some people believe football is a matter of life and death. I'm very disappointed with that attitude. It's much more important than that.'

After his much-mourned death from a heart attack in 1981, Liverpool erected the Shankly Gates at Anfield as a permanent memorial to the man who made the club what it is today. His ashes were scattered over the pitch.

There will always be a corner of an English field that is forever Scottish, and forever Shankly's – the man of the people. We will never see his like again.

From one unforgettable Scot to another, this time Tommy Docherty, who could have stepped off the boards of the Glasgow Empire. The man has always been a walking, talking headline-maker, and these days is an in-demand after-dinner speaker who is as funny as any comedian in the land.

Docherty made news wherever he went as a manager, and he went to a lot of places. As he once famously said, he had more clubs than Jack Nicklaus. Let's count them: he played with distinction for Celtic, Preston and Arsenal before starting a managerial career with Chelsea, followed by adventurous assignments with Rotherham, Queen's Park Rangers (twice), Aston Villa, Oporto in Portugal, Hull City, in Glasgow as Scotland manager, Manchester United, Derby County, Sydney Olympic, Preston, South Melbourne, Wolves and, finally, Altrincham. I make that sixteen clubs and one national team. If he took as many on the golf course he would be disqualified.

Half the time, Bill Shankly did not know he was being funny. Tommy Docherty, by contrast, was usually intentionally hilarious and played it for laughs even at the gravest moments in his roller-coaster career. As we've already heard, the Doc was sacked by Man United for his affair with Mary Brown, the wife of the club physiotherapist. Tommy takes up the story: 'When Mary and I gave the news to her husband Laurie that we had fallen hopelessly in love he was standing in his kitchen with a bread knife in

Tommy Docherty, Manager of the Month with Man United in 1974, says: 'Look what I got for George Best. Not a bad swap.'

Copyright © popperfoto.com

his hand. I decided to lighten the moment by saying, "While you've got that in your hand, Laurie, do us a favour and cut me a sandwich."'

Only the Doc could be that outrageous. Only the Doc would have shared the story. He simply could not resist being the conduit for anecdotes that were usually hilariously, and sometimes hideously, funny.

The Doc was on a shortlist of two for his first coaching job in football at Chelsea. He told the club's directors, 'If you appoint the other man, you won't get a coach. You'll get a hearse.'

He was sacked by Aston Villa chairman 'Deadly' Doug Ellis in 1970 with Villa jammed at the bottom of the Second Division after he had bought and sold enough players to fill a cattle truck. Tommy came out with one of his classic quotes after his departure from Villa Park: 'Doug Ellis told me that he was right behind me. I said I preferred it if he were in front of me, where I could see him.'

We've had the Shanklyisms. Now for the Dochertys . . .

Talking of an England full-back: 'I've seen milk turn faster.'

Told by a chairman that one hundred thousand wouldn't buy his centre-forward, Tommy replied, 'Aye, and I'm one of those hundred thousand.'

When Ray Wilkins was skipper at Manchester United, Tommy told radio listeners, 'The only time he goes forward is when he has to toss the coin.'

One morning during the Doc's spell in charge at Old Trafford, he walked into the medical room to find striker Stuart Pearson on the treatment table.

'What's wrong with you?' he asked.

'I've got a bad back,' said Pearson.

'Not to worry, son,' said Tommy. 'Manchester City have got two bad backs.'

Tommy was once asked if, while he was manager at Man United, he had received any death threats. 'Only the one,' he replied, deadpan. 'A supporter wrote to me and said that if I picked goalkeeper Paddy Roche again, he'd kill himself.'

Docherty can be devastating in his criticism of some current managers. 'They're so negative these days,' he said, 'they should be working for Kodak.'

When taking over as Wolves manager in the bleak mid-1980s at Molineux he said, 'I have just opened the trophy cabinet and two Japanese prisoners of war came out.'

Talking scornfully about cricket and cricketers: 'Och, that's the only game where players can actually put on weight while playing.'

After Mark Wright had limped off during a match, Tommy said, 'He's so injury-prone he'd pull a muscle appearing on *A Question of Sport*.'

The Doc on football-club directors: 'An ideal board would be made up of just three directors – two dead and the other dying.'

Making an after-dinner speech at a time when George Best was in the news for one of his drunken escapades: 'I'm sorry George could not be with us here tonight. He was launching a ship in Belfast and wouldn't let go of the bottle. We tried to get Ron Atkinson as a substitute, but he's in mourning for his hair-stylist . . . who died in 1956.'

I finish this chapter with the manager who was probably the greatest character of them all: of course, the irrepressible Cloughie. John Sadler, an exceptional sports columnist with the *Sun*, was Boswell to Brian's Dr Johnson, and I am grateful to him for his contribution to the following collection of quotes from the great man.

On how he rated himself: 'I wouldn't say I was the best manager in the business. But I was in the top one.'

On the influx of foreign players in the British game: 'I can't even spell spaghetti, never mind talk Italian. How could I tell an Italian to kick long balls? He might kick mine.'

On not getting the England manager's job: 'I'm sure the England selectors thought if they took me on and gave me the job, I'd want to run the show. They were shrewd, because that's exactly what I would have done.'

On too many managers getting the sack: 'If a chairman sacks the manager he initially appointed, he should go as well.'

On the importance of passing to feet: 'If God had wanted us to play football in the clouds, He'd have put grass up there.'

Explaining his Old Big 'Ead nickname, after he had been awarded the OBE: 'Yes, I own up to being big-headed on occasions. I call myself Old Big 'Ead just to remind myself not to be.'

When told that he earned three times more than the Archbishop of Canterbury, Cloughie replied: 'Quite right. The Derby ground is always full, while the churches are three-quarters empty.'

On Martin O'Neill, who played under him at Forest: 'If he'd been French or Swedish, he'd have walked the England job.'

On the streaker who raced across the pitch during a Derby County game against Manchester United: 'The Derby players have seen more of his balls than the one they're meant to be playing with.'

On dealing with Roy Keane: 'I only ever hit Roy the once. He got up, so I couldn't have hit him very hard.'

On his drinking problem: 'Walk on water? I know most people out there will be saying that instead of walking on it, I should have taken more of it with my drinks. They are absolutely right.'

On dealing with a player who doubts his orders: 'We talk about it for twenty minutes and then we decide I was right.'

Asked to comment on Sir Alex Ferguson's failure to win two successive European Cups, Cloughie said: 'For all his thoroughbred racehorses, knighthoods and championships, he hasn't got two of what I've got. And I don't mean balls!'

On England goalkeeper David Seaman: 'That Seaman is a handsome young man but he spends too much time looking in his mirror, rather than at the ball. You can't keep goal with hair like that.'

On Eric Cantona's infamous karate kick at a fan when playing for Man United at Crystal Palace: 'I'd have cut his balls off.'

Ah, Cloughie. They definitely threw away the mould after making him. Yes, he managed all right.

You've gotta laugh

It was Christmas 2001 and the good fairy visited Gerard Houllier in his office at Anfield. 'Monsieur Houllier,' she whispered. 'You are a good man and it has been decided that you can have one wish as a special Christmas present.'

Houllier had no hesitation in saying, 'Ah, *ma chère*, you are a dream come true. Ever since I moved here to Liverpool I have wanted them to build a bridge from Merseyside to France. I hate flying and the British trains are so unreliable. If you build a bridge for me, I could drive.'

'Oh no, *monsieur*,' said the fairy in an apologetic tone. 'That is an impossible wish to grant. It would be too difficult a task even for me with my magic powers. Please try again.'

Houllier thought hard before saying, 'I have a player in my team who should score more goals. Can you make him into a twenty-goals-a-season player? His name is Emile Heskey.'

The fairy recoiled and raised her hands. 'OK, how many lanes do you want on your bridge?'

Hark who's talking

Glenn Hoddle:
'OK, so we lost, but good things come from it – negative and positive.'

John Aldridge:
'You can't wait until you're a goal down at half-time, an away goal at that, before you throw the gun at them.'

Joe Royle:
'I don't blame individuals. I blame myself.'

Bill McGarry:
'I'm not going to name names, but our number nine had a stinker.'

Howard Wilkinson:
'I am a firm believer that if you score one goal, the other team have to score two to win.'

John Bond:
'I promise results, not promises.'

Ron Greenwood:
'Football is a simple game. The hard part is making it look simple.'

Ian Holloway:
'My day didn't start very well. The Holloway household had to have our dog put down unfortunately, but that's life. I've just said to the lads: "You're born and you die on a date. You've got to work on the dash in the middle."'

Jack Charlton:
'I'm not going to have a go at the referee, but he was a complete twerp.'

Gerard Houllier:
'You cannot say my team are not winners. They've proved that by finishing fourth, third and second in the last three years.'

Martin O'Neill:
'Anybody who is thinking of applying for the Scotland job should go and get themselves checked out by about fifteen shrinks.'

Kevin Keegan:
'There's a slight doubt about only one player, and that's Tony Adams, who definitely won't be playing tomorrow.'

Brian Clough:
'If a fox is completely brilliant he finds a hole and hides. If he's discovered, he's dug up and thrown to the hounds. But a football manager doesn't even have a hole to hide in.'

Bobby Robson:
'Well, we got nine . . . and you can't score more than that.'

Gordon Lee:
'I don't know how some of our players can look themselves in the mirror after that performance. Perhaps they should do it with their eyes closed.'

Bill Nicholson:
'We were complete rubbish and I hope the players feel guilty when they collect their wages this week.'

David Pleat:
'The manager we want at Tottenham has to fit a certain profile. Is he a top coach? Would the players respect him? Is he a nutcase?'

Dave Jones:
'Carlton Palmer covers every blade of grass, but he has to because his first touch is that crap.'

Malcolm Allison:
'You're not a proper manager until you've been sacked.'

Don Revie:
'I've been in this game too long to start slagging off the referee, but I'll be very surprised if he's got a father to confess to.'

Vic Buckingham:
'Once the first whistle goes you're in the hands of your players, and there are some players in my team that I wouldn't trust with my crockery.'

Stan Cullis:
'Any player of mine who gives less than one hundred per cent on the pitch knows that he is best off going into the other dressing-room at the final whistle.'

Gordon Strachan:
'We're fourth in the table! Fourth. Just hope nobody gets nosebleeds. I'm going home and I'm going to sit with a bottle of Coke, a packet of crisps and stare at the Teletext League tables for three hours.'

Joe Mercer:
'There are many things wrong with the clubs, and we managers, also with the players, administrators, the media and – definitely – the referees. The only thing with which there is nothing wrong is the game itself.'

6 Who's the *Real* Bastard in the Black?

Anybody who volunteers to be a football referee needs his (or her) brains tested. I would rather stand starkers in a swarm of bees with nectar spread on my privates than expose myself to the ridicule, the tantrums and the contempt that referees have to face at all levels of the game. All I will say is that those people brave – or foolish – enough to take the job know what they're letting themselves in for, because there's no way they can please all the people all of the time.

A good referee can make a game, and a bad one can break it. I've seen some real clowns in my time, and have wondered where they've left their guide dogs. I remember standing on the Kop for one match watching the referee have such a shocker that somebody shouted, 'For f***'s sake, Ref, send *yourself* off.' Come to think of it, it might have been me who shouted it.

Ever wondered when the first chant of 'Who's the bastard in the black?' was heard? I can be specific with the answer. It was back in the early days of the game when a prominent referee rejoiced in the name of Segal Richard Bastard. He had played for England before switching to refereeing, and almost caused a riot in the 1878 FA Cup final when he turned down a goal because of offside.

There have been many more referees accused of not having a father since then, and the pressure on them has increased because of the mountains of money now at stake in the major matches. The game has changed out of sight since I first started watching and playing it back in the 1940s, and contentious things like tackling from behind and charging the goalkeeper have, so to speak, been kicked out.

Referee David Elleray took a modern-day look at the brutal 1970 FA Cup final replay in which Chelsea beat Leeds 2–1 at Old Trafford. As he watched the video horror show he worked out that he would have produced six red cards and twenty yellows in the course of the match. But in the original game not a single name was taken during a battle featuring such kick-yer-granny legends as Billy Bremner, Jack Charlton, Norman 'Bites Yer Legs' Hunter, Johnny Giles and Ron 'Chopper' Harris.

Elleray was always an open-minded referee, and on another occasion he agreed to take part in a 1980s television trial in which he was miked-up during a match between Millwall and Arsenal. Away from football he was a teacher at the lah-di-dah Harrow public school. Arsenal skipper Tony Adams was out of the say-it-as-you-see-it Essex school. The FA officials monitoring the microphone experiment almost choked on their cigars when they heard the following discussion after Elleray (incorrectly) ruled that the ball had not crossed the goal line following an Arsenal corner:

Adams, in Essex-speak: 'That was over the line. You're a f***ing cheat, Ref!'

Elleray, in his received pronunciation: 'You may call me useless, but I am *not* a cheat.'

It was decided there and then that television viewers should not be allowed to hear the sort of exchanges that are part and parcel of the professional game. Told what the microphone had picked up, Adams said later: 'Yeah, well I do get a bit emotional. But it *was* over the f***ing line.'

At least David Elleray communicated with the players. I always preferred the walkie-talkie refs like Gordon Hill, Norman Burtenshaw, Roger Kirkpatrick, Clive Thomas, Tommy Dawes,

Jim Finney and Arthur Ellis. At least they were human and chatted to the players. But today all the humour has gone out of the refs and they are like a bunch of bloody robots.

But think how much harder it is for today's referee to note the name of the player he is booking. There are so many foreign players with tongue-twisting names that the refs must feel they have wandered into a school for languages. How do they know when they are not being sworn at when players such as Kuntz, Turdo, Fukal, Pinas and Bernt Haas give them their names?

During an after-dinner gig I sat next to a Premiership ref, who shall be nameless, and he opened my eyes to just how difficult it is to be in charge of a top football match these days. The refs are under the all-seeing eye of an assessor – usually a former referee – who marks them out of a hundred, making only negative comments and never praising what he might do right. It's a Big Brother system that I think puts too much pressure on the poor old ref. As I write, they are talking of bringing in TV replays to help with some decisions. The sooner the better. The only thing that matters is getting it right. It works perfectly well in cricket and rugby, so why not football?

My favourite fictional referee story always triggers laughter on Merseyside, and sums up the sort of strain the man in the middle is under:

A referee arrives at the Pearly Gates and St Peter is waiting to give him his entry examination. 'Have you ever done anything stupid in your lifetime?' he asks.

'Yes, I have,' the referee confesses. 'I was in charge of the Merseyside derby between Liverpool and Everton at Anfield. With the score 0–0 I gave Everton a last-minute penalty at the Kop end. In truth, I made a mistake and it should not have been a penalty.'

'I see, my son,' says St Peter. 'When exactly did this happen?'

The ref looks down at his watch, and replies, 'About thirty seconds ago.'

Love them or loathe them, referees are key people in the game and without them I would not have the following hilarious stories for my collection.

Those of us who have, um, played away in our time will sympathise with the Brazilian referee who almost literally got his knickers in a twist. He reached into his pocket for a red card and, like a magician, managed instead to hold aloft the red lace panties that he had earlier removed from his mistress. His face was almost as red as the card he finally managed to flourish in front of the offending player he was sending for an early bath. It gets worse. His wife was among the spectators, and it was reported that she was giving *him* his marching orders. Interviewed after the 2004 match in Anama, the referee allegedly confined himself to one word to reporters: 'Knickers!'

A referee who was also a police inspector gave the Manchester City players their pre-match instructions in the dressing-room before a League match, and then asked if there were any questions. Mike Summerbee, the joker in the City pack, put up his hand and asked, 'When are you going to catch Lord Lucan?'

I've heard of hungry footballers but this is ridiculous . . . Fernando d'Ercoli got so angry when the referee sent him off while playing for Pianta against Arpax in a match in Italy in 1989 that he snatched the red card, stuffed it in his mouth and ate it!

And referees can get hungry, too . . . Romanian ref Petronel Enache went on a hunger strike in protest at his treatment by his local federation. He was forty-eight hours into his farcical fast when it was agreed that his request to be promoted to First Division status would be assessed. Bet that was a weight off his mind.

Swansea referee Tom Reynolds was the busiest man on the pitch during an FA Cup tie between Chelsea and Birmingham City at Stamford Bridge. Birmingham won 1–0 but had five players booked. After the game, the ref found his car was blocked in by the Birmingham City team coach. He went to the dressing-room, poked his head round the door and asked, 'Where's your coach driver?'

'Bloody hell, ref,' replied a Brummie voice. 'Don't tell me you're going to book him as well.'

Toothless Tiger Nobby Stiles was in trouble with referee Pat Partridge when Man United were playing Burnley in a floodlit match at Old Trafford. Nobby kept snapping away at the heels of Burnley centre-forward Andy Lochhead, and was twice quietly warned 'watch it' by the ref. Partridge, good enough to referee in the 1978 World Cup finals, finally lost his patience, and took out

A sight guaranteed to unite all supporters: the referee taking a tumble. This happened in a 1990 First Division match between Coventry and Liverpool. For the poor old man in black it can be reffing hell.

his book in the second half after Nobby's badly timed tackle had sent Lochhead tumbling.

'But it's the floodlights, Ref!' Nobby protested. 'They shine in my contact lenses and I can't see a bloody thing.'

Partridge was unimpressed and started to write Nobby's name in his book, misspelling it 'Styles'.

Nobby peered over his shoulder and said, 'You can't even get my bloody name right.'

Partridge countered, 'I'm surprised you can read with the floodlights shining on your contact lenses.'

Nobby gave a toothless grin. 'Nice one, Ref,' he said. 'Spell it how you like.'

Women referees and assistants are beginning to make the breakthrough into professional football. Wendy Toms, the first woman referee to handle a top professional game, made it difficult not to go down the road to innuendo when she said in a pre-match interview, 'If the players want to make it hard for me, I am happy to make it twice as hard for them.'

Arthur Ellis became known throughout the land as the man with the whistle on television's *It's a Knockout*, but he was much better known in football as one of the world's leading referees. He always handled matches with good Yorkshire humour, and when he and Clown Prince Len Shackleton got together on the same pitch there was certain to be laughter to go with the action. One occasion that Shack recalled was when he was playing for Sunderland's 'Bank of England' team alongside that powerful Welsh international centre-forward Trevor Ford.

Early in the game Shack slipped a pass through to Ford, who fired a first-time shot into the net. Referee Ellis saw his linesman's flag go up and ruled it offside.

Shack – making sure that Ellis was in earshot – called out, 'That was a bloody lousy decision, Trev.'

Arthur cocked a deaf 'un and waved play on. He knew there would be an opportunity to have his say.

Sure enough, a few minutes later, Shack had a scoring chance, but he screwed the ball wide.

Ellis laughed as he shouted to Shack, 'And that was a bloody lousy shot.'

Honours even between two of the game's great characters.

In another match Ellis had a run-in with Shack, when Len kept querying his decisions.

'Listen, Shack,' said an exasperated Ellis, 'who's refereeing this match – you or me?'

Shack, the wittiest footballer of his generation, countered, 'Neither of us.'

Was there ever a quicker thinker on the pitch than 1966 World Cup master Bobby Moore?

A referee was once knocked cold when a hard-driven ball smashed into his face during a League match at West Ham. The game was in full swing and Bobby had the presence of mind to go immediately to the prostrate figure of the ref, pick up his whistle and blow it as he summoned the trainer to treat the poleaxed official.

And Bobby used to tell another true, hair-raising story:

West Ham were playing at Newcastle on a very windy day. In fact I can never remember playing at St James' when it wasn't windy. Anyway, on this particular day I was summoned to the centre-circle for the coin-tossing ritual by referee Ricky Nicholson, who had a striking head of shining black hair. I lost the toss and we had to play into the teeth of the vicious wind. Newcastle quickly had us under pressure and forced an early corner. The referee came and took a position just a few feet from me. I looked at him and then gave a classic double take. He was as bald as a coot. I was fighting to keep a straight face, and he knew it. He gave a dry smile and said quietly, 'It's OK,

Bob. It's in my pocket. I washed it last night and don't want it blowing off and getting dirty!'

It was difficult to pull the rug from under him, then.

Referees have to be on their toes from the moment of the first whistle. My fellow thespian Vinnie Jones will vouch for that. He was on the end of the fastest-ever booking in British football when he was yellow-carded just three seconds into Chelsea's game against Sheffield United at Stamford Bridge. He whacked into United's Dane Whitehouse straight from the kick-off. 'One thing's for sure,' Vinnie said later, 'it was not a booking for a late tackle!'

The previous record had been a booking after five seconds when Manchester City's man mountain Niall Quinn was cut down to size by a thumping tackle against Wimbledon. The perpetrator was, um, Vinnie Jones.

Vinnie, sent off twelve times during his League career, surpassed himself in a celebrities soccer match in Hollywood. He was called off the substitute's bench and was back fifteen seconds later after being red-carded for an instant tackle that deserved an 'X' certificate.

But even Vinnie was a slow coach compared to Walter Boyd, whose contribution to Swansea's game against Darlington in 1997 lasted zero seconds! Boyd was summoned into the game as a substitute with seven minutes to go after Swansea had been awarded a free-kick. He got involved in some argy bargy with Darlington defender Martin Gray and was ordered off before the free-kick could be taken. Clive Wilkes, the referee who sent Boyd packing, was so proud of the instant dismissal that he has had the moment captured in a weather vane fitted on the roof of his house. It shows him flashing a red card. Sort of taking Boyd's name in vane.

I am told that a non-League player was ordered off as the referee blew the whistle to start the match. He was red-carded for shouting, 'F*** me, Ref, that was loud.'

A game has to be abandoned if a team is ever down below eight players. It happened once in the UK when the 2002 Sheffield United–West Brom match was called off after eighty-two minutes with United having three players red-carded and another injured. They were losing 3–0 at the time, and the result stood.

But this was tame compared to a Second Division match in Paraguay in 1993. Referee William Weiler set a new benchmark when he ordered off – wait for it – *twenty* players. It all started to unravel after he had sent two home players for an early bath. Their team-mates staged a protest, and then fist-fights broke out all over the pitch. Weiler reacted by ordering off the entire home side and nine of the visitors.

The British record for one-team bookings in a UK match is held by Mansfield. Ten of their players had their names taken for 'ironically' applauding the referee after he had awarded a late penalty in an FA Cup tie at Crystal Palace in 1963. They slow handclapped the referee's decision, with only the goalkeeper missing out. Palace scored from the spot to take the game to a replay. Mansfield won it 7–2, obviously going like the clappers.

There has been no more instantly recognisable referee in world football than Italy's Pierluigi Collina, whose dome-shaped bald head and Popeye staring eyes made him stand out like an arrival from Mars. Czech midfielder Radoslav Latal must have wondered if Collina had extrasensory powers when he showed him the red card in the last minute of the Holland–Czech Republic Euro 2000 match in Amsterdam. What made it so unusual was that Latal was on the substitutes' bench at the time, but Collina's antennae had picked up the abuse he was shouting after he had awarded a disputed penalty.

While playing for Santos in a club match in Bogota, Pele was ordered off by the referee after reacting to a series of savage tackles on him.

Pele was back in his dressing-room removing his boots when the message came, 'Get on the pitch, quick.' His sending-off had so enraged the huge crowd that had come to watch him play that spectators were setting fire to their seat cushions and throwing them on to the pitch. A watching bigwig from the Colombian Football Association decided that the referee should be replaced and Pele brought back on! In effect, the referee was sent for an early bath.

Managers often swallow their suspicions that referees in European cup matches have been 'got at', rather than risk legal fisticuffs with Sue, Grabbit and Run. But dear old Brian Clough never used to mince his words. If he thought a referee was bent, he made sure everybody knew his opinion whether or not he was right. There was the famous case when Derby lost a European Cup tie 3–1 against Juventus in Turin, with the German referee making a string of *questionable* decisions. Cloughie, incandescent with rage, told the waiting journalists after the game, 'I will not talk about any cheating bastards. Got it? No cheating bastards will I talk about.' I wonder what Cloughie would have made of the referee in Ecuador who added *twenty-two* minutes of injury-time to a League game – yes, *twenty-two* minutes. He elected to blow the final whistle within seconds of the visiting team scoring a winning goal. It was later discovered that he was standing for election to a political post in the city of the team that, with his timely assistance, won the match.

No fewer than thirty-three referees were arrested in an investigation into match fixing in South Africa in 2004. The inquiries started just weeks after a coach had been shot dead by a referee for disputing his decisions. Undercover police carried out the probe in what was coded Operation Dribble. Ah, the Beautiful Game.

Belgian referee Jacques Temmerman was waiting for a free-kick to be taken during a match between Young Stars Eeklo and FC Zelzate when a spectator ran on to the pitch and pulled down his shorts and jockstrap. Temmerman, his face as red as one of his cards, retired there and then from refereeing.

I used to love the comments from Ron Atkinson before he got caught out talking while his brain was not in gear. Once, when manager of Man United, he was asked for his views on a referee whose performance had been, to say the least, weak. 'I never comment on referees,' said Big Ron, 'and I'm not going to break the habit of a lifetime for that prat!'

Players in a match in Finchley, north London, were giving the referee a lot of verbals, and questioning his parentage. Suddenly the ref ran off the pitch, went to his car and came back wielding an axe. The players scattered and the game was abandoned. I wonder if Chopper Harris was playing?

Talking of Ron Harris, who was out of the Tommy Smith, Norman Hunter, retaliate-first school of defenders, reminds me of when Prince Philip was at Stamford Bridge watching as a guest in the directors' box. With a rascally twinkle in his eye, he asked the Chelsea chairman Brian Mears why Harris was known as 'Chopper'. At that precise moment the referee booked Harris for one of his infamous chopping tackles. 'Ah,' said the Prince. 'I see.'

The Nigerian League came to a standstill in 2000 when the referees went on strike because they were fed up with not being shown enough respect on or off the pitch. Bloody hell, if referees were that sensitive in England we would never get a ball kicked.

Life was hell for Spanish referee José Garcia Aranda after he had handled the World Cup qualifier between Uruguay and Paraguay in Montevideo in 2001. Señor Aranda was held responsible by the home fans for Uruguay's shock 0–1 defeat, and he had to be smuggled out of the ground. While checking in his luggage at the airport for the flight home he was fairly disturbed to find himself queuing with five hundred Uruguay fans who had arrived for a local flight. Security guards had to rescue him as the supporters mobbed and attacked him, and once again he was smuggled away, but not before one of the guards had been injured by a stone meant for Aranda. Who'd be a ref?

A referee in Malawi was arrested and taken to hospital for a drugs and alcohol test after his bizarre handling of a League game. He had awarded both teams two penalties . . . and punched a photographer. The game was held up for twenty minutes after one of his four penalty decisions because of rioting fans. Peace was restored only after police had fired tear gas into the crowd.

Even more eccentric were the decisions of Belgian referee Amand Ancion, who was reported to have been diagnosed as having psychological problems after he had awarded five penalties and handed out nine yellow cards in the barmy 6–6 draw between Westerlo and Genk in 1999.

The same referee's weird decisions got former Manchester United midfielder Ronnie Wallwork so worked up that Ronnie – allegedly, of course – put his hands round Ancion's throat. Wallwork, on loan to Royal Antwerp, was at first banned for life from football, but the suspension was quickly lifted when the controversial incident was properly investigated. United centre-half Danny Higginbotham, also on loan and involved in the same fracas, had his year's ban dropped.

Ancion was later sacked after disallowing what TV cameras

John Barnes is testing whether the ball is properly cooked. It was Liverpool who were well done at the end, losing 3–4. It's a funny old game.

Copyright © popperfoto.com

proved to be a valid goal in a Belgian League game between Mouscron and Charleroi. He had blown his final whistle.

A referee in Peru red-carded three Miners' Union players as they protested over a twice-taken penalty in a League match against Sport Boys. The rest of the Union players walked off in protest. They were persuaded to return to the pitch after twenty minutes of argument, but then the referee decided he'd had enough and refused to restart the match. It was abandoned with a minute still left of the first half. The Miners said the ref was the pits.

They do tend to be a bit eccentric in South America. Perhaps it's something to do with all that coffee. Olaria were playing Bangu in a Brazilian League match when the referee awarded a disputed penalty in the eightieth minute. It was so disputed that

133

the Olaria players refused to let it be taken. They formed a wall across the goal, with their coaching staff and substitutes joining in. The referee waved his red card at all of them and abandoned the match.

Some other Brazilians accused Welsh referee Clive 'the Book' Thomas of playing God during their opening match in the 1978 World Cup finals in Argentina. Brazil were being held 1–1 by Sweden with the match into its last seconds when Zico headed Nelinho's corner past goalkeeper Ronnie Hellstrom. But Thomas had blown for time as soon as the corner had been taken and so disallowed the goal. Technically, he may have been correct ('The amount of time is at the discretion of the referee'), but the Brazilians went bananas and asked who the hell he thought he was to split time to such a fraction.

Last they saw of him, Clive was walking across the River Taff.

It beats me why referees are not instructed only to blow the final or half-time whistle when the ball is dead. But then, what do I know? I've only been watching the game for more than fifty years.

There was a wonderful scene played out in the middle of a pitch in Cumbria in 2003 when Askam United waited for the kick-off to their local League match against Furness Rovers. What followed could have come out of a *Little Britain* script. The start was delayed for fifteen minutes while *two* referees stood in the centre-circle arguing as to which of them should take charge. The dispute boiled over to the point where they stood face to face, blowing their whistles at each other. They had been double booked for the match and neither would back down. Finally, the players got fed up with waiting and found another referee, and the two warring officials were relegated to running the lines. You wait for one ref, and two arrive at the same time.

The referee of a Norwegian match was replaced at half-time because he was legless. He had turned up drunk, and could not keep up with the play. One of the coaches said, 'I think he must have been seeing two balls because he hardly got a single decision right.' Apparently the ref complained about the decision to send him off, saying, 'I'm not as think as you drunk I am.'

The referee of a midweek match in Gloucestershire was upset when one of the players called him a 'wanker', so he booked him and reported him to the Football Association. It turned out that the man he booked was his boss, who fired him from his print-works job. Bossy boots!

In the same game, the referee booked another player, who was a work colleague. He took revenge by spraying the ref with cleaning fluid. I am not making this up! It all came out in a tribunal report, when the referee got a six-thousand-pound pay-off award for wrongful dismissal. I bet the boss saw red!

One of the worst decisions I've seen in modern times robbed Tottenham of an obvious goal at Old Trafford in the winter of 2005. It was a case of 'Now is the winter of our discontent' for Spurs as the beautifully named referee Mark Clattenburg waved play on after the ball had clearly crossed at least a yard over the United goal line. Every action replay and newspaper photograph showed goalkeeper Roy Carroll pulling the ball back from way over the line after he had been caught napping by a hopeful forty-five-yard punt from Pedro Mendes. It was all very well to blame the ref, but what the hell was his linesman – sorry, his assistant – doing? 'There was nothing I could have done differently apart from run faster than Linford Christie,' he was reported as saying. It wasn't speed he needed; it was sight. Blimey, my old granny could have seen it was miles over the line. I think Mike Bassett would have been on the pitch telling him where to stick his flag.

You may never have heard of a referee called Bill Harper, but he was the first to be caught out by a camera. He was refereeing the 1932 FA Cup final between Newcastle and Arsenal at Wembley when, in the thirty-eighth minute, Magpies winger Jimmy Richardson crossed a ball that had clearly gone over the Arsenal dead-ball line before he connected. The Arsenal players stopped playing and waited for a goal-kick to be awarded. Newcastle centre-forward Jack Allen nonchalantly steered the ball into the net unchallenged for what, amazingly, was to be an equalising goal.

Everybody in the ground seemed to know the ball had gone out of play, with the exception of Mr Harper. It is a sign of the discipline of teams in those days that not a single Arsenal player protested when the referee pointed to the centre-circle. They just got on with the game in a mood of dumb disbelief. These days the ref would no doubt have found himself covered in pizza!

Referee Harper said after the match: 'Take it from me, it was a goal. As God is my judge, the ball was in play. I don't care what other people may say. I was eight yards away, and know what I saw.'

Oh dear, not only a wrong decision but caught out telling porkies, too. Mr Harper became the first referee to be proved wrong by modern technology. Although pretty archaic by the standards of today's instant action replays, film from British Movietone News proved beyond doubt that the ball had gone out of play before it was crossed. The camera also clearly showed that the referee was a good twenty-five yards behind the play.

Jack Allen scored a second goal for Newcastle eighteen minutes from the end to clinch a disputed victory. Nobody said 'Lucky Arsenal' after this match as their dream of a double died, and they eventually finished second in the League to Dixie Dean's Everton, too.

Modern referees often seem to have had a humour bypass. There was that lovely incident in Scotland when the ref dropped his cards. Paul

Gascoigne – of course, it had to be Gazza – was standing alongside him. He picked up the cards and held the yellow one above the ref's head to show him he had been booked. It was hilarious. But what did the ref do? He promptly held up the yellow card to Gazza for 'showing dissent'. He was not showing dissent; he was displaying something that's all but disappeared from the game – a sense of humour. Gazza didn't deserve a card but a standing ovation.

Now for something that I'm surprised doesn't happen much more often: a referee whacking a player! Take a bow Macau official Choi Kuok-kun. He was seen live on television punching a Hong Kong player who objected to being sent off by kicking the ball at him. They started fighting and had to be separated by other players. Blimey, that's like the postman biting the dog. Kuok-kun's reward was to be banned from refereeing for life. I think it's called the Order of the Boot.

Mihai Macovei, chairman of the Moldovan team Roso Floren, found a new way of protesting against a referee's decision. He raced to the car park, jumped in his Jeep and drove on to the pitch honking the horn. The ref reacted by abandoning the game, and the barmy boss and his club were handed a massive fine. Jeepers!

I blow the final whistle on this collection of referees stories with one you just couldn't make up: the referee who sent *himself* off. (Remember my shouted advice from the Kop in the introduction to this chapter?) Andy Wain decided he was the one who had to go during a Sunday League match between Peterborough North End and Royal Mail AYL. Wain lost his temper when the Peterborough goalkeeper protested over one of his decisions, threw down his whistle and went eyeball to eyeball with the goal-keeper.

'Suddenly I realised that I was in the wrong for reacting the way I did,' said the ref. 'So I decided I had to go.'

He walked off for an early bath, leaving the players with no option but to abandon the game.

There's only one way to sum it all up . . . Reffing hell!

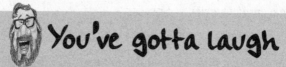

You've gotta laugh

A referee decides he has to make a quick getaway after a match in which he sends off four players and gives two controversial penalties. He drives too quickly, crashes coming round a bend and is thrown through the windscreen on to the road.

By coincidence, the car following him is driven by one of the players he sent off, and he stops to see if he can help. He finds that the referee is in a bad way and makes a 999 call on his mobile.

'I think the referee's dead,' he shouts down the phone in panic. 'What can I do?'

'Calm down,' says the operator, used to dealing with emergencies. 'First of all, go and make sure the referee is dead.'

The operator hears a choking sound and the cracking of a neck bone. Then the player returns to the mobile.

'OK,' he says. 'I've made sure he's dead. Now what should I do?'

Hark who's talking

Kevin Keegan:
'I'm not trying to make excuses for David Seaman, but I think the lights may have been a problem.'

Sir Bobby Robson:
'We haven't scored, which means you haven't got a chance of winning.'

Alec Stock:
'We would have won if we'd taken our chances and they'd missed theirs.'

David Pleat:
'We came here with a game plan but parked it at the gate.'

Terry Neill:
'It's not for me to make excuses, but they had all the luck and we had none.'

Bill McGarry:
'We had three key players out injured, and the ground did not suit us at all. But I am not going to make excuses.'

Tommy Docherty:
'We were at sixes and sevens and as we only have eleven players in our team it's no wonder we looked confused.'

Bob Stokoe:
'I'm not going to hide behind excuses, but their second and third goals should have been ruled offside, and the fifth came after we were down to ten men.'

Theo Foley:
'The dice were stacked against us.'

David O'Leary:
'If we had taken our chances, we would have won – at least.'

Ronaldo:
'We lost because we didn't win.'

Peter Beardsley:
'When I was seventeen I could have signed for Newcastle, but I decided I was better off at Carlisle. I'd had a good drink that night.'

John Terry:
'We did not come here to play for a draw, or any other result.'

Vic Buckingham:
'But for their winning goal, we would have gone on to win comfortably.'

Harry Catterick:
'You don't have to be a mathematician to know we'd have won if we'd scored more goals than them.'

Ted Bates:
'I would like to turn the clock back ninety minutes, and I'm sure we'd come up with a different time.'

Bertie Mee:
'You can plan for most things in football except that for which you can't plan.'

George Graham:
'The one thing I didn't expect is the way we didn't play.'

7 Sweet, Sweet FA

The Football Association is, quite rightly, fiercely proud of its past. Never call it the English FA. It's *the* Football Association, because it was the first football organisation in the world when founded back in the nineteenth century. It is responsible for running and supervising all grassroots football in England, as well as the national team and the FA Cup. It accomplishes an enormous amount of good for the game, but to go with the historical achievements there are also a lot of hysterical moments.

Nothing was funnier than the disclosures in the summer of 2004 of sexual shenanigans in the ivory tower of the FA, involving a beautiful secretary called Faria Alam and the England team coach Sven-Goran Eriksson. That was juicy and scandalous enough, but it got even better and more farcical when it emerged that Ms Alam was also giving her favours at the same time to the chief executive of the FA, Mark Palios. One of the funniest parts of the exposé was when Ms Alam revealed how she had sat at a restaurant table playing footsie with *both* of her admirers, with neither of them knowing that she was bedding the other. It gave a whole new meaning to good with both feet.

Palios resigned over the affair, while smooth Sven survived, but with his long-term partnership with the hot-blooded Nancy Dell'Olio once again taking a shot between the bedposts. It had been rocked and shocked early in Sven's England career when he was caught in a fling with the Swedish temptress Ulrika Jonsson. I hear that at the most passionate moment Sven threw his arms up as if he had scored (which he had) and shouted, 'Eureka, Ulrika!'

Sven somehow managed not to blink behind those rimless glasses of his when Ms Alam shared with the nation – through an exclusive interview with the *News of the World* – that before following her upstairs to bed he insisted on stacking the dish-washer. It is this attention to detail that has earned him such a big reputation as a coach, and makes him a real polisher in my book.

What is it with the England manager's job? It seems to act as some sort of aphrodisiac. As I mentioned earlier, Bobby Robson was linked with two redheads in the rumour-mongering media when he had the job, and Sven's sex life attracts as much attention as his coaching. Blimey, Mike Bassett was like a vicar on Viagra

Gimme five. Sven is either showing how many goals England have scored against Germany or how many times he scored with the Football Association secretary.

when he had the England job, but his leg-over attempts always ended in farce rather than fulfilment.

Careful scrutiny of the FA's leadership of the game since its formation in 1863 reveals many bumbling and bungling moments, but the Sven–Palios scandal was the first time they had been caught with their trousers down. Of course, now that red-blooded Scouser Brian Barwick is in charge dignity and decorum will return to football's corridors of power.

Jimmy Greaves gave me a grand insight into the often barmy world of international football when we met at a sportsmen's dinner. He said:

We called the FA officials in my playing days the Blazer Brigade. They would turn up for international matches and tours in their England blazers, old fogeys living in the fantasy world that they were part and parcel of the football team. I remember seeing an FA councillor fall asleep at an after-match banquet with his head perilously close to the soup de jour. He was so startled when nudged awake by his neighbour that he knocked the soup into his lap, much to the merriment of we players who were watching the pantomime from an adjoining table.

A ritual that many of the officials looked forward to after the banquets following international matches was the exchange of gifts. Our FA representatives used to receive things like cut-glass decanters and expensive cigarette boxes, and would give in return ropy FA ties and cufflinks. There was one overseas banquet when our FA spokesman stood up to say thanks for the beautiful gifts received. When it came time for him to present the reciprocal gifts he got urgent sign language from a colleague pointing out that the cufflinks and ties had been left behind in the hotel. 'On behalf of the Football Association,' our man said, then hesitating as he got the message, 'I'd like to give you our, um, apologies . . .'

Of course, the players just collapsed, as we did at another function when our representative stood up, wiping his mouth with the tablecloth that he had mistaken for his napkin. He then made a long, rambling speech, and kept prolonging it because he interpreted our laughter as appreciation of his feeble jokes. What was amusing us so much was the fact that his flies were undone.

Ah, sweet, sweet FA. Here are a few more crackers about the well-meaning people who run – I almost said *ruin* – our great game.

Ron Flowers, the powerful, blond Wolves midfield anchorman, went through a three-match England tour without getting a game. But after every match one elderly blazered official came up to him and congratulated him on his performance. His parting shot at the end of the tour was, 'We will be hearing a lot of you, Bobby.' He had gone through the entire tour convinced that Ron was Bobby Moore.

It is not only the English FA that is overloaded with buffoons. How about this tale from the Valleys told by flying Tottenham winger Cliff Jones:

The Welsh squad for a 1960s international match in Eastern Europe gathered at Heathrow Airport. There were ten officials, manager Dave Bowen, trainer Jack Jones, eight pressmen and ten players. It was the usual old story that some clubs were not releasing their players until the last minute, and it had been arranged for two other players to join us the next day just a few hours before the kick-off.

Anyway, our flight was called and there was the usual panic rush from the duty-free shop to the departure gate. This was in the days before they gave you individual seats as you checked in, and there was quite a bit of jostling and jockeying as we filed on to the plane; you know, with players trying to get with mates and Welsh FA officials getting as far away from us as possible.

Finally, we were all seated, with the exception of one FA councillor, an old boy who was standing in the aisle looking lost. The flight had been overbooked. After several minutes the air hostess announced that the last person named on the checking-in passenger list would have to leave the plane and catch a later flight, and as we were going behind what was then the Iron Curtain these were hardly flying every five minutes.

She read out the last name: 'Mr G. Reece. Would Mr G. Reece kindly leave the aircraft?' This was Gil Reece, one of our ten players.

There was a long silence as we all waited for one of the officials to surrender his place so that Gil could stay on board. A couple of them fidgeted uncomfortably in their seats, and the man standing in the aisle tried to make himself invisible while he waited for a vacant seat. Nobody moved. Eventually, with a gesture of disgust, Gil Reece got up and walked off the plane. We did not know whether to laugh or cry as we took off with nine players.

Later, one of the WFA officials approached the pressmen who were sitting just behind me at the rear of the plane. They were expecting an explanation or perhaps a confession. They leaned forward, notebooks at the ready. 'I feel it only right that I should mention this, boys,' the official said. 'I thought one of you might have had the decency to volunteer to stay behind.'

On a later Welsh trip Newcastle goalkeeper Dave Hollins joined the squad at the airport for an international match in Greece. He was wearing his Newcastle club blazer. In the bus taking them from the departure lounge to the aircraft he stood next to a Welsh FA councillor who took a close interest in Dave's attire. 'What badge is that?' he asked.

'Newcastle United,' said Dave.

'Really,' said the old boy, who was wearing his Welsh FA blazer. 'Where are you off to then?'

'Greece, of course,' said Dave, trying not to look too puzzled. 'That's a coincidence,' the official beamed. 'So are we!'

One bigwig in the Football League and the FA used to butcher the English language. He was chairman of a disciplinary committee and told the player standing before him, 'I can promise you a pathetic hearing.'

After a crowd riot at his club, he told a press conference, 'I will not rest until we get sanitary restored to the game.'

Another of his classic gaffes was to say at an after-match banquet, 'I would like to thank our Bulgarian hosts for their wonderful hospitality.' The England squad were in Romania at the time.

He once revealed that there was 'perfect harmonium' in the England dressing-room, and on another occasion stood on the beach in the millionaires' paradise of Acapulco and – thumbs tugging at his braces – said in all seriousness, 'Gi'e me Blackpool any day.'

I don't know whether to laugh or cry at this story of how the Football Association managed to cock up our preparations for the 1950 World Cup finals. The FA saw fit to organise a goodwill tour of Canada at the same time as the finals in Brazil, and then ummed and ahhed when Manchester United requested that none of their players should be considered because they had arranged a trip to the United States.

Manager Walter Winterbottom, battling against this blinkered club-before-country attitude, almost had to get on his knees to have first choice for the World Cup. As it was, he had to go to Brazil without England's most famous player, Stanley Matthews, who was sent on the totally meaningless Canadian trip as a footballing ambassador. Special arrangements had to be made to fly him down to Rio for the finals, but he still arrived after England had won their opening match 2–0 against Chile. Winterbottom wanted to play Stanley in the second game against the United States at Belo Horizonte, and Sir Stanley Rous argued the case for him with the chairman of the selectors, a Grimsby fish merchant called Arthur Drewry, who had been appointed the sole selector – sole, geddit? – for the World Cup. 'My policy is that I never change a winning team,' the dogmatic Drewry said dismissively.

On one of the blackest days in English footballing history, England were beaten 1–0 by the United States, with Stanley Matthews among the spectators. It was like leaving Wellington on the bench at Waterloo. What a way to run an international team. Bloody hell, it makes Mike Bassett seem like a genius.

Skipper Billy Wright told a story from that 1950 World Cup tournament which captures the amateurish way in which we approached international football. Nobody had bothered to check what food the hotel would serve in Brazil, and the players complained that they could not eat it because it was too spicy. Manager Walter Winterbottom decided the only way round the problem was to go into the hotel kitchen and do the cooking himself.

Talk about head cook and bottle washer! Can you imagine Sven in a chef's hat? 'Swedish meatballs, anybody?'

Chairmen and directors provide a lot of laughs, mostly unintentionally, in the village world of football, where everybody knows everybody else's business. Dave Sexton, one of the most revered coaches in the game, who managed Chelsea and Man United and has been a long-time member of the England backroom team, recalled:

Manchester City were playing Everton in the semi-final of the FA Cup, and sneaked a 1–0 victory. Dear old Albert Alexander, who was then City club chairman, made his way slowly from the directors' box to the dressing-room, where the players were celebrating with champagne. Manager Joe Mercer called for order. 'Our chairman would like to make a brief announcement,' he said.

'Congratulations, lads,' said Albert, 'You've done us proud. The final at Wembley will make the club a lot of money, and then we'll be able to go out and buy some good players.'

The only sound heard in the suddenly deathly quiet dressing-room was that of old Albert trying to remove his foot from his mouth.

Ipswich Town were struggling down in the depths of the old First Division, and their Old Etonian chairman John Cobbold was asked if the club was in crisis. 'Crisis? Mr dear boy, what we consider a crisis here is when we run out of white wine in the boardroom. *That's* a crisis.'

Cobbold, from the famous Suffolk brewery family, was one of the most lovably eccentric people ever to take the boardroom chair. He once gave his skis to a train driver after returning to Ipswich station from a holiday in the Swiss Alps. 'Well, you tip a cab driver, why not a train driver,' he said with a shrug.

Jackie Milburn, then manager of Ipswich and deeply concerned about a losing sequence, buttonholed the chairman during another train journey, from Liverpool Street to Ipswich. He talked long and passionately about where he thought things were going wrong, and the plans he had to put matters right. As he was building up to the punchline that he would need some money to spend in the transfer market, he felt confident because he was convinced he had the chairman's total attention. He was about to quote the price for a player when Cobbold pointed out of the train window and exclaimed, 'Just look at the size of the bollocks on that bull!'

Cockney comedian Tommy 'You Lucky People' Trinder was, of course, one of football's great personalities when he was chairman of Fulham. He once walked into the dressing-room at Craven Cottage to find trainer Frank Penn massaging a greyhound.

'What's that?' asked Tommy. 'Our new centre-forward?'

'It's a greyhound,' said the trainer.

'I can see that,' said Tommy. 'But what's it doing in here?'

'It belongs to Charlie Mitten [Fulham's outside-left],' explained Frank. 'We're getting it in the mood for tonight's big race.'

Charlie came in at that point. 'There you are, Guv'nor,' he said to the chairman. 'Been looking for you to tell you about the dog. Do yourself a favour and get your money on it. The dog's running at Slough this evening, and it's a cert.'

'But you can't train greyhounds here,' protested Tommy.

'I think you'll have to turn a blind eye just this once,' said Charlie, famous for his persuasive tongue. 'All the players have got their money on it, and it'll upset them if we upset the dog.'

Tommy gave up arguing and fished into his wallet. 'Here's a fiver,' he said. 'Put it on him to win.'

The dog trailed in last.

Tommy had a notice put up in the treatment room that read: 'Two legged animals only'.

Jimmy Hill was also closely associated with Fulham, first as a player and later as chairman. On the famous day that he headed five goals in Fulham's 1–6 victory at Doncaster, Tommy Trinder decided to follow tradition for anybody scoring three or more goals and present him with the match ball. The Doncaster chairman was not so keen on the tradition, and insisted on Tommy paying him for the ball.

Jimmy was never lost for words on the pitch. He once took a throw-in and directed the ball back towards his own defence. A woman supporter leaned over the wall and shrieked at him, 'Not that way, you fool. *That* way!'

Jimmy glanced round to see she was standing with a man he presumed to be her husband. 'Don't nag at me,' he said. 'Nag *him*!'

Talking of nags, Jimmy joined in a hunt in the Midlands in the bad old days of fox hunting. He was sitting astride his mount waiting for the hunt to start when his horse loudly broke wind. Jimmy was talking to an aristocratic lady at the time and, rather embarrassed, said, 'I'm sorry about that, your Ladyship.'

'Oh, that's all right,' she said. 'I thought it was the horse.'

Football League chairman Keith Harris (not the one who makes a living with his hand up Orville's arse) and chief executive David Burns were forced to resign in the wake of the ITV Digital failure that cost League clubs millions of pounds. As the resignations were being announced, Burns was overheard whispering to Harris, 'Just think, we're giving the asylum back to the lunatics.'

Sir Alan Sugar, once owner of Tottenham and still with a considerable stake in the club, condemned footballers with such ferocity that what was intended as criticism nose-dived into a Victor Meldrew-style rant. Here's what he said while publicising his *The Apprentice* TV show:

> *Football players are scum, total scum. They're bigger scum than journalists. They don't know what honesty or loyalty is. They're the biggest scum that walk on this planet and, if they weren't football players, most of them would be in prison, it's as simple as that. Do not believe a word that comes out of their mouths. All they're interested in is themselves. And, if something doesn't go right, they'll go behind you and stab you in the back. If you ever had to go into the trenches and you had to rely on people, don't ever rely upon footballers.*

I think Sir Alan Sugar should say what he means, instead of perching on the fence like that. I know, I'm fired!

How mad can the game get? Uri 'the Bender' Geller and Michael 'Wacko' Jackson took it to the limit of absurdity when they paraded together at that famous football outpost of Exeter City, giving the impression that they were ready to forge a boardroom partnership. Exeter players started practising moonwalking the ball into the net, and stirred their half-time cuppas with bent spoons. Of course, it all came to nothing and it was rumoured that Jacko lost interest because he considered the Football League 'Never Never Land'.

Michael Knighton gave us one of the biggest laughs in football when he attempted, and almost succeeded, to take over Manchester United in 1989 with a bid of twenty million pounds, something like 5 per cent of its value just a decade later. Within hours of the announcement of his takeover offer, he made a right prat of himself by putting on a tracksuit, going out on the pitch and juggling the ball in front of a packed Old

Here's a meeting of great sporting minds. This is me with Ian Wright, Ryder Cup captain Sam Torrance and Scouse snooker ace John Parrott before *A Question of Sport*. Everybody expected me to know sweet FA, but I am a walking dustbin of knowledge on football, and even more so on boxing. I could bore for Britain.

151

Trafford. It was like somebody taking over the Royal Philharmonic and then sitting at the piano and playing chopsticks. That was when the alarm bells started ringing that he might be a brick or two short of a full house. He bought Carlisle United instead, and made a right pig's ear of it. In my opinion (and, of course, I am not referring to Mr Knighton) football clubs in need should bear in mind the old saying, 'Beware a geek bearing gifts.'

You have to go abroad to find the biggest nuts in football administration. Few could compete with Atletico Madrid president Jesus Gil in the madness stakes. He was virtual owner of the club across two decades and hired and fired no fewer than thirty-nine managers, including Ron Atkinson, who described him as 'completely barmy'.

He used to become incandescent in defeat, once threatening to machine-gun all his players and another time telling them to swim home after a loss in the Canary Islands. After having a pacemaker fitted, he shouted during an after-match interview, 'They can stick my heart up their arses.' Jim Royle would have been proud of that one.

At the time of his death in 2004, Gil was contesting a prison sentence for allegedly siphoning money from city funds into the coffers of his football club while he was mayor of Marbella.

His colourful language is sadly missing from the game. He came out with this classic after his star player Hugo Sanchez had refused a new contract: 'He is as welcome at my club as a piranha in a bidet.'

But even Jesus Gil would have to take a back seat in the potty stakes to Luciano Gaucci, overlord of Italian club Perugia. When South Korea knocked Italy out of the 2002 World Cup he went apoplectic because one of his players, Ahn Jung-Hwan, scored the winning goal. Gaucci vowed he would never kick another ball for his club. He then signed Al-

Saadi Gaddafi, son of the charming Libyan president, and topped that by bringing in a new fitness trainer: none other than Ben Johnson, the sprinter who was stripped of his Olympic gold medal for taking drugs. Gaucci had been impressed by the way Johnson trained that other well-known man of honour(!), Diego Maradona!

Gaucci has campaigned for mixed football teams, and vowed that he would sign the best women footballers he could find to play for Perugia. Can you imagine how many players will be trying to get early baths?

A racehorse owner and breeder, he has threatened his players that instead of being fined for poor performances they will have to muck out his stables. He sounds like just the sort of bloke who would hire Mike Bassett to manage his team. Must get my application written: 'Dear fellow nutter . . .'

Have you heard the one about the entire team that was arrested? An amateur team in Brazil were going through their usual training ritual in a small park backing on to a row of houses. Suddenly Judge Rosemeire Conceicao arrived waving a warrant for their mass arrest, and police took them off to the local nick. It turned out that Conceicao lived in one of the houses adjoining the park, and the footballers had ignored her warnings to stop kicking the ball against her walls. She claimed they had caused structural damage and also disturbed her privacy. The team were released on bail, and the judge announced that she would be suing them privately.

Sounds to me like they needed a referee rather than a judge.

We stay in Brazil for another cracker that will never – and I am prepared to bet an FA Cup final ticket on this – be emulated by the likes of Alex Ferguson, Arsène Wenger or even the arch-exhibitionist Jose Mourinho. Paulo Mata, excitable coach of Itaperuna, was so incensed by a series of what he considered bad refereeing decisions against his team that he stripped off and streaked across the pitch during a League game in

Rio. Two policemen got to him and, um, covered his tackle. Then, giving an after-match interview live on television, the amazing Mata suddenly dropped his shorts and mooned millions of viewers. Now that really is football my arse!

You've gotta laugh

Manchester City manager Stuart Pearce gets a letter from a teenage Iraqi begging for a trial. He invites him over from bomb-blitzed Baghdad, and gives him a run out for the reserves against the first team. The young Iraqi runs rings around the City defenders on his way to a hat-trick, and Pearce decides to sign him.

The boy asks if he can talk to his parents first, and the manager hands him his mobile.

'Mamma, I've just scored a hat-trick in my trial and Manchester City want to sign me,' he says, hardly able to contain his excitement. He then realises his mother is crying. 'What's the matter, Mamma?' he asks. 'Why are you crying?'

'Today has been the worst day of our lives,' she says. 'Worse even than when Bush was raining his bombs down on us. Your father has been shot, your sister kidnapped, and the house ransacked and burned.'

'I'm so sorry, Mamma,' he says. 'I should not have left you. But I so wanted to do well in this trial in Manchester.'

'I know, son,' she replies. 'But why did you have to bring us with you?'

Hark who's talking

Steven Gerrard:
'I've got a good record there – played one, won one. Hopefully it will be the same after Saturday.'

Kevin Keegan:
'People will say that was typical City, which really annoys me. But that's typical City, I suppose.'

Jack Charlton:
'I've seen them on television on a Sunday morning most days of the week.'

Howard Wilkinson:
'If they hadn't scored, we would've won.'

Ian Rush:
'You sometimes open your mouth and it punches you straight between the eyes.'

David Beckham:
'Me, volatile? Well, I can play in the centre, on the right and occasionally on the left side.'

Mark Draper:
'I'd like to play for an Italian club, like Barcelona.'

Derek Johnstone:
'He's one of those players whose brains are in his head.'

George Best:
'Most of the things that I've done are my own fault, so I can't feel guilty about them.'

Alan Ball:
'I'm not a believer in luck, although I do believe you need it.'

Graham Taylor:
'Shearer could be 100 per cent fit, but not at peak fitness.'

Bill Nicholson:
'I will not name my team until just before the kick-off, but it will definitely be unchanged.'

Dick Graham:
'We will be playing four–four–three. And if you can make sense of that, you're a better man than I am, Gunga Din.'

Johnny Giles:
'I'd rather play in front of a full house than an empty crowd.'

Elton John:
'For all of us at Watford, this is a tremendous headache lifted off our shoulders.'

Barry Venison:
'I always used to put my right boot on first, and then obviously my right sock.'

Glenn Hoddle:
'We don't want to put a timescale on the player's injury. He could be back in four weeks, but we'll reassess in three weeks' time.'

Bobby Gould:
'We are really lucky this year because Christmas falls on Christmas Day.'

Terry Butcher:
'The beauty of cup football is that Jack always has a chance of beating Goliath.'

Arsène Wenger:
'It is farcical Sol has been cited. It seems to me we are living in farciland.'

Jason McAteer:
'They call me Trigger at Sunderland because I once went into a pizza parlour and was asked whether I wanted it sliced into four or eight slices. I told them four because I couldn't manage eight slices.'

Paul Gascoigne:
'I've had fourteen bookings this season – eight of which were my fault, but seven of which were disputable.'

Ade Akinbiyi:
'I was watching the Blackburn game on TV on Sunday when it flashed on the screen that George Ndah had scored in the first minute at Birmingham. My first reaction was to ring him up. Then I remembered he was out there playing.'

8 Oops, All My Own Work!

Let's kick-off this chapter with the funniest goal I ever saw; probably the most hilarious one ever scored in a top-level football match. The place: Anfield. The date: Saturday, 9 December 1967. The match: Liverpool against Leeds United.

We (that's Liverpool, in case you're wondering) were leading 1–0 through a Roger Hunt goal, and there were just a few minutes to half-time when Leeds goalkeeper Gary Sprake, unchallenged, gathered a harmless through-ball. This was at the Kop End, and we groaned because a promising attack had fizzled out to nothing. Now a groan from the packed Kop – twenty-five thousand of us squashed together in conditions that would have brought complaints of overcrowding from sardines – sounded like the bellow of a battalion of bulls. Suddenly the groans gave way to roars of disbelief followed by helpless laughter. Sprake had managed to throw the ball over his shoulder and into the corner of his own net. It was as if the Kop choir had decided as one man to pray. We were literally brought to our knees, almost crying with laughter and unable to cheer a goal that had put us completely in charge of a vital First Division game.

The knots of Leeds fans scattered around the ground were stunned into gaping silence. They were struggling to believe the evidence of their own eyes. All the Leeds players had been running away from Sprake as he went to throw the ball out, and they looked round when they heard the roars. Leeds centre-half Jack

Charlton said to referee Jim Finney, 'What the flaming hell's happened?' Or words to that effect.

Finney, one of those fantastic old-fashioned referees who used to have a chat and a chuckle with the players and treat them like adults, said, 'Well, Jack, your goalkeeper has just thrown the ball into his net, and I am awarding Liverpool a goal.'

It has entered the mists of football myth that the Liverpool fans immediately broke into choruses of 'Careless Hands', the Des O'Connor song that was top of the pops at the time. That's not true, because we were too busy laughing to be able to sing at the time. No, poor old Gary had to wait until he ran out for the second half to be greeted by the Kop in full voice singing the song, geed up by the club disc jockey who played it over the Tannoy.

From that day on, Sprake was always welcomed by the song whenever he played at Anfield. He took it well, and rose above the king-size blunder to win thirty-seven Welsh international caps and a stack of medals with Don Revie's Leeds.

There's only one other match when I've heard a goal greeted with gales of laughter. This time it was on the other side of Stanley Park at Goodison. It was the 1969 Merseyside derby, and Everton's faithful left-back Sandy Brown threw himself full length to score with a spectacular diving header. Unfortunately for him, it was into his own net. The blue half of Goodison went into silent mourning, and we in the visiting red half laughed and laughed and laughed until we were as red as the shirts of our heroes. The goal often pops up on videos and DVDs of classic footballing gaffes. See it if you can, and take special note of the policeman crossing behind the goal as the ball goes into the net. He is leading the applause. Obviously a red-blooded boy in blue!

These two classic own goals provide the perfect foundation for my collection of stories about goofy goals that needed no input from the opposition.

All goalkeepers like an early touch of the ball, and Arsenal right-back Lee Dixon decided to oblige David Seaman with a back pass

Mike Bassett is lost for words when interviewer Stuart Hall asks him, 'Why is your centre-forward in the nick when he should be here representing his country?' This was the last interview ever on the old Wembley pitch.

from thirty-five yards in a 1991 match against Coventry at Highbury. He struck the ball beautifully and it floated into the top-right corner over the head of the Flying Ponytail. The match was not even a minute old.

The previous year Arsenal had conceded an even quicker own goal, this time with John Lukic between the posts. Steve Bould shanked comically past his goalie with just thirteen seconds of the match gone against Sheffield Wednesday at Hillsborough. Football my arsenal!

There must be something about Wednesday. Alan Mullery, the old Fulham, Tottenham and England warhorse, was in the record books for a long time with the quickest own goal, also against the Sheffield team. He sent a pass back from twenty yards towards goalkeeper Tony

Macedo after less than thirty seconds of a 1961 First Division match. Macedo was not expecting it and watched like a statue being shat on by pigeons as the ball rolled past him and into the net. Fulham had started badly, and it got worse: they lost 6–1.

But nobody in the world has had the ball into his own net quicker than Torquay defender Pat Kruse. Cambridge kicked off the Fourth Division match at Plainmoor on 3 January 1977, and Ian Seddon wellied the ball high into the Torquay penalty area. Centre-half Kruse rose like a salmon in the middle of the Torquay defence and headed the ball beautifully into his own net. Time: eight seconds! It gave a whole new meaning to Kruse control.

Remember Tony Hateley, who was a fantastic header of the ball in the mid-sixties? He scored buckets of goals with his head for Notts County, Aston Villa and Chelsea before Bill Shankly shelled out what was then a club record hundred grand to bring him to Anfield. Liverpool went four games away without scoring a single goal after Hateley's trumpeted arrival. Then, on 28 August 1967, the big man – built like a brick out-house – broke his duck with a bullet header at Highbury. Trouble was it was into his own net from an Arsenal corner, with the ball crashing past our goalkeeper Tommy Lawrence, who understandably had been keeping his eye on the red-and-white shirts of the Gunners. Talk about beware the enemy within.

Hateley used to fall over his own two feet as if he were Jimmy Riddled, and – admittedly not in the best of taste – we nicknamed him Douglas Bader, because he was great in the air but useless on the ground. His son, Mark, was nearly as good a header and much better with the ball at his feet. But here's a little fact for you to chew on: Mark was capped 32 times by England and netted a total of 178 League goals during his career; his dad, without a cap to his name, scored 211.

Has there been a dafter own goal than the one concocted by Aston Villa against deadly rivals Birmingham City in a Monday-night Premiership match at St Andrew's on 16 September 2002?

Villa's Olof Mellberg took a throw-in out on the right and aimed it at his goalkeeper Peter Enckelman, who was all alone in the penalty area. The Finnish international stuck out his foot to control the ball, with his eye on where to put it next. The ball appeared to brush against his studs and rolled merrily on its way into the Villa net, with Enckelman chasing it like a drunk trying to make it to the bar before last orders. Bloody hell, my granny could have stopped it.

Villa fans wanted to throw up, and a Birmingham supporter was arrested for charging on to the pitch and making Sherman tank hand gestures in front of the embarrassed Enckelman. It's rumoured that he later tried to throw himself under a bus, but missed it.

Another Villa player, centre-half Chris Nicholl, had a fairly eventful game against Leicester City in a First Division match at Filbert Street on 20 March 1976. He put the ball into his own net twice and scored two conventional goals in a 2–2 draw. Both teams no doubt voted him man of the match!

The uncrowned king of own goals has to be Belgian defender Staf Van Den Buys. During Anderlecht's 3–2 win over Germinal Ekerren in 1996 he scored all of the Anderlecht goals ...while playing for Ekerren. I wonder if he got the match ball?

How about this for a unique own goal – one shared between two players! Leicester City defenders Jim Milburn and Jack Froggatt went for the same ball in a First Division match against Chelsea at Stamford Bridge in 1954. They connected simultaneously with their attempted clearance kicks and the ball went zooming into their own net. Two into one does go!

That great character Jimmy Greaves, with whom I have shared after-dinner speaking dates, told me this hilarious story about when he was a young goalscoring sensation with Chelsea:

We were playing Everton in a League match when a long shot slipped under the body of our England international goalkeeper Reg Matthews. Reg scrambled up and chased after the ball, hotly challenged by our big, bold captain Peter Sillett, who thought he had a better chance of clearing it. They pounded neck and neck towards our goal. Reg won the race and then, instead of diving on the ball, elected to kick it away. He pivoted beautifully and cracked the ball dead centre – straight into the pit of Peter's stomach. The ball rebounded into the back of the net, and Peter collapsed holding his stomach, groaning. The rest of us players collapsed holding our stomachs, laughing. It was one of the all-time unforgettable goals that belonged in a Carry On Football *script.'*

Arsenal left-back Dennis Evans was in possession in front of his goal at Highbury when he heard the referee's final whistle at the end of a First Division match against Blackpool in 1955. He casually walloped the ball into the net, only to discover that the whistle he'd heard had come from the terraces. It was an unexpected consolation goal for Blackpool, who were beaten 4–1.

Here's a nomination for one of the pottiest games ever played. Barbados went into their 1994 Shell Caribbean Cup tie against Grenada needing to win by two clear goals to qualify for the next round. The local rules were that if the teams were level after ninety minutes, the game would be decided by a sudden-death goal. Barbados were leading 2–0 when, with seven minutes to go, Grenada scored.

A 2–1 scoreline would have meant Grenada going through. Unable to break down Grenada's massed defence, Barbados deliberately put the ball into their own net to make it 2–2. They were banking on getting the sudden-death goal. This woke up Grenada to the fact that if they scored at *either* end before the ninety minutes were up they would go through.

So the crowd watched the bizzarre spectacle of Barbados defending both goals in the last desperate minutes. They lined up on their opponents' goal line to stop them putting the ball into their own net, and kept defenders back to protect their own goal. They managed to keep Grenada out at both ends and eventually won on a sudden-death goal. A funny old game? No, barmy fits the bill better.

Ronnie Whelan scored some lovely goals for Liverpool. Sadly, one of the best was into his own net against Manchester United at Old Trafford in 1990. He chipped it perfectly from twenty-five yards and it dipped over the startled goalkeeper Bruce Grobbelaar and under the crossbar. We won't blame 'Grobb the Grabber' for that one.

Mind you, Whelan did not feel as bad as Jamie Carragher, who once headed two own goals while playing against United in a match at Anfield. Take it from me, the glory did not go to his head.

Own goals are not always funny. Often they are heartbreakers, like the one Steven Gerrard scored in the 2005 Carling Cup final at the Millennium Stadium.

Gerrard is one of the few modern English players who can look the great ghosts of our footballing past in the eye, and he is Liverpool red-blooded through and through. His attempted clearance went from his head into the Liverpool net to bring Chelsea

163

back from the dead, just as it looked as if the Reds were going to nick the trophy. Then Chelsea's manager, Jose Mourinho, did something you would never have caught the likes of Shankly, Paisley, Busby and Nicholson doing: he started taking the pee out of the Liverpool supporters, who had been taunting him. Quite rightly in my view, he was sent off. It was the sort of unacceptable and irresponsible behaviour that could have incited crowd trouble. Mourinho said that he was having a go at the press rather than the spectators, but I don't think too many reporters were sitting among the Liverpool fans.

Mourinho is quite a character, and has brought colour – as well as his old overcoat – to the English game. But a little bit of humility would not go amiss. As good as Jose seems to be at the managing lark, I have to say that with the billions that Roman Abramovich is tossing into the bottomless Chelsea pit I reckon that even Mike Bassett could put together an all-conquering team, and he would not resort to having a go at the fans who put their hard-earned money into the game.

Was Mourinho right to make that finger-to-the-lips gesture? No way, Jose.

There's a line in Oscar Wilde's *The Importance of Being Earnest*: 'To lose one parent, Mr Worthing, may be regarded as a misfortune; to lose both looks like carelessness.' I wonder if this quote came to Sunderland manager Howard Wilkinson's mind when they gave away not one, not two, but *three* own goals in eight minutes in a 3–1 Premiership defeat to Charlton in 2003? I'll tell you this, if Mike Bassett had been in charge of the team there would have been blood on the dressing-room walls.

Leicester City defender Frank Sinclair took the art of scoring own goals to a new plateau in August 1999. In two Premiership matches right at the start of the season – against Arsenal and Chelsea – he guided the ball into his own net in the last minute of each game. His first goal gave Arsenal victory; the second robbed Leicester of a win.

Sinclair was at it again in March 2002 when his back pass from thirty yards left goalkeeper Ian Walker floundering and sailed into the net to give Middlesbrough a 1–0 win against Leicester. My Mike Bassett tactical advice if I'd been Leicester manager would have been, 'Don't give Sinclair the ball.'

Tottenham were coasting to victory against Crystal Palace at White Hart Lane in 1973 when eccentric left-back Cyril Knowles casually kicked the ball back over his head from forty yards, taking it for granted that goal-keeper Pat Jennings would collect it. Jennings had not had a shot to save all afternoon and was on gardening duty at the front of the penalty box, replacing divots in the pitch. He scurried back to try to catch the ball but could only watch as it bounced into the empty net. Nice one, Cyril!

Jimmy 'Mr Portsmouth' Dickinson is the only England player to have scored an own goal during a World Cup finals match. He headed the ball into his own net during extra-time of England's 1954 group game against Belgium, and it gave the Belgians a 4–4 draw. Jimmy, who won 48 England caps and played a then record 764 League games for Pompey, was mortified. 'It was the only time I got on the England scoresheet,' he said, 'and it was the only own goal of my career.'

When John Barnes sent a free-kick for England crashing against the bar in an international against Greece it rebounded into the net off the goal-keeper. Without hesitation, all of the English reporters in the press box awarded it to Barnes rather than attempt to dictate the name of the goalie whose own goal this rightfully was. His name? Spiros Economopoulos. Were they being economical with the truth about Economopoulos? No, just saving precious space.

The first own goal at Wembley was conceded by England goalkeeper E.H. (Teddy) Taylor in a Home Championship international match against Scotland in 1924. He left his goal line to clear the ball but managed only to punch it into his own net to give the Scots a 1–1 draw in the first international staged at Wembley.

Teddy played for the Huddersfield team that won a hat-trick of League championships, but he was a Scouser. So on Merseyside we can claim to have had the first player to make Wembley his own, so to speak.

Did you know that Tony Adams is the only player to have scored for and against England in the same match? He scored an own goal against Holland at Wembley in 1988 and then went upfield to head an equaliser to salvage a 2–2 draw.

This was around the time when Adams was drinking himself silly, as he has confessed while making a courageous recovery from alcoholism. Once he drove into a wall while out of his head, and the joke shot around the village world of football that he was trying to get the wall to move back ten yards.

Sadly, I cannot make reference to own goals without mentioning the one scored by Colombian defender Andreas Escobar in the 1994 World Cup finals. Escobar put the ball past his own goalkeeper on the way to a shock 2–1 defeat against the United States, and he paid for it with his life. Just days after the team had made an early return home, Escobar was shot and killed in his home town of Medellin. Rumours have never gone away that it was a contract killing ordered by a bookmaker who had lost a fortune to people betting on a US victory. Witnesses of the murder said that he was shot six times and that after every shot his assassin shouted, 'Goal!' *Not* funny.

This is me and *Corrie* star Bradley Walsh on location in Brazil during the making of the *Mike Bassett* movie. Bradley was on Brentford's books before deciding it was easier to get laughs than goals. He went for a five-mile run every day while working on the film. After a week we had to send a car to bring him back to the film set. He was thirty-five miles away.

South African supporters must have felt like shooting defender Pierre Issa when he managed to score two own goals against France in the 1998 World Cup finals. The game was played on the ground of Olympique Marseille, which just happened to be his club. You would have thought he would have known which way to kick.

Finally, an own-goal story that sounds as if it could have been a Monty Python sketch, yet it is absolutely true. Adama, champions of Malagasy (formerly Madagascar), beat Stade Olympique de l'Emryne by a world-record 149–0 in a League match on 31 October 2002. That's amazing, but even more astonishing is the fact they were *all* own goals! Olympique repeatedly put the ball into their own net in protest at a referee's decision that they claimed cost them the championship.

The Beautiful Game my arse!

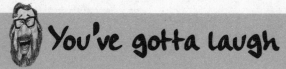 # You've gotta laugh

Just before manager Claudio Ranieri parted company with Chelsea he bumped into Sir Alex Ferguson at a service station on the M6.

They got talking about the transfer market and the players they had bought and sold.

'That-a Juan Sebastian Veron who I-a bought from you,' Claudio said, in his Spaghetti Junction English, 'I-a call him my-a wonder player.'

Sir Alex was surprised, because he thought Veron had been a disaster at Stamford Bridge. 'Why d'ye call him yer wonder player?' Alex asked in his distinctive Glaswegian accent.

'Well,' said Claudio, 'every-a time he-a plays, I-a wonder how I-a let-a you con me into buying him.'

Hark who's talking

Vinnie Jones:
'Winning doesn't really matter as long as you win.'

Peter Reid:
'Magnifico . . . or whatever they say in Paris.'

Mick McCarthy:
'I was feeling as sick as the proverbial donkey.'

Steve Coppell:
'At the end of the day it's all about what's on the shelf at the end of the year.'

Peter Shilton:
'If you stand still in this game there's only one way to go, and that's backwards.'

Kevin Keegan:
'England have the best fans in the world. Scotland's are second to none.'

David O'Leary:
'Achilles tendon injuries are a pain in the butt.'

Ray Wilkins:
'Unfortunately, we keep kicking ourselves in the foot.'

Ron Wylie:
'I don't believe in setting targets, because the only target I have in mind is beating Stoke City.'

Steve Lomas:
'Germany are a very difficult team to play . . . They had eleven internationals out there today.'

Bobby Robson:
'In a year's time, he'll be a year older.'

Mitchell Thomas:
'All that remains is for a few dots and commas to be crossed.'

Dean Holdsworth:
'The only way we'll [Wimbledon] be going into Europe is if the club splash out and take us all to Eurodisney.'

Tommy Burns:
'In Glasgow half the fans hate you, and the other half think they own you.'

Bryan Robson:
'It wasn't going to be our day on the night.'

Mark Viduka
'I'd not be bothered if we lost every game as long as we won the League.'

Glenn Hoddle:
'I've never heard a minute's silence like that one.'

Kenny Dalglish:
'As I've said before and I've said it in the past . . .'

Denis Law:
'There's no way Ryan Giggs is another George Best. He's another Ryan Giggs.'

Steve McMahon:
'I'd kick my own brother if I had to. That's what being a professional footballer is all about.'

Dave Bassett:
'You have got to miss them to score sometimes.'

Mike Channon:
'We won, so I'm over the moon, Brian . . . um, sorry, Barry.'

Norman Whiteside:
'The only thing I have in common with George Best is that we come from the same place, play for the same club and were discovered by the same man.'

Stan Bowles:
'The referee's a wan . . . plonker.'

Steve Perryman:
'There were a lot of boots flying around out there today and a few players lost their heads.'

Carlton Palmer:
'I said to the players before the start, "Just go out and give it one hundred per cent. I am not asking for any more than that."'

Glenn Hoddle:
'Well, at the end of the day, that's it. It's all over.'

9 World Cup Willies

Imagine if we had been awarded the 2006 World Cup in the UK, and that somebody came up with the bright idea that we should call the mascot World Cup Willie! Sounds ridiculous, doesn't it? But that's exactly what they did in 1966 when the finals were memorably staged in England. It illustrates just how times and tastes change. If Willie was suggested now to represent the country the not-so-bright spark who came up with it would quickly be shown the door. 'You can't have the fans shouting, "Wave your Willie in the air,"' I can hear the FA chief executive saying at the planning committee meeting. Then again, with the recent history of the Football Association, perhaps it would be considered appropriate.

Willie was a lovable little cartoon lion, and the very first commercial mascot for a World Cup. Every ball-kicking kid in the country had to have one, so parents were nagged into buying the doll version. If you were wise enough to keep it in good nick, they are worth a bob or two nearly forty years on.

I was earning my daily bread as a plasterer on building sites when the World Cup came to England, and it caused a real buzz on Merseyside because we hosted some of the North West Group games at Goodison, in conjunction with Old Trafford. The four teams drawn in the local group were the champions Brazil, Hungary, Bulgaria and Eusebio's Portugal.

But what should have been a feast and a festival of football turned into a bloody war zone. You should have seen the kicking that went on, and I don't mean of the ball. The great Pele was tackled out of the tournament, and if the same non-contact rules had been applied then as now few matches would have finished with more than nine players on each side.

Goodison staged a quarter-final that produced one of the most memorable matches in history. Little North Korea, who had already shocked Italy out of the tournament, rushed into an unbelievable 3–0 lead against Portugal. Enter Eusebio. The Black Panther gave the most brilliant individual performance that has ever been seen on the Goodison pitch, and that took some doing on the home ground of Dixie Dean, Tommy Lawton and Alex 'the Golden Vision' Young. Almost single-handed, he pulled Portugal back into the game with a haul of four goals in thirty-two minutes that propelled the Portuguese to a breathtaking 3–5 victory. For a while it led to a new saying on Merseyside: when a team came from behind to win we would say, 'They've been Eusebioed.'

You can imagine the jokes that were flying around Liverpool. 'You say BO . . . Yes, you are stinking the place out.' And, of course, the tiny Koreans were quickly nicknamed the Diddy Men (copyright the great Ken Dodd), and we had great fun getting our tongues round names like Pak Doo-Ik and Li Dong-Woon.

But nothing that happened on the pitch in 1966 could compete in the humour stakes with the farce that almost turned the build-up to the finals into a national disgrace. The Football Association managed to lose the bloody World Cup – the priceless Jules Rimet Trophy – before a ball had been kicked. It was nicked while on show at a stamp exhibition in Westminster just weeks before the kick-off of the greatest football show on earth. We did not know whether to laugh or weep. We are fairly infamous up on Merseyside for finding things that fall off the backs of lorries, but we would not be stupid enough to put sport's most precious trophy within easy reach of outstretched hands.

A massive police and public hunt was launched, and just when it looked as if the cup had disappeared into the smelter's pot it was unearthed by a dog called Pickles, who sniffed it out from its hiding-place under a bush in Norwood, south London.

Pickles and his owner Dave Corbett collected a £6000 reward and a man who had demanded a £15,000 ransom for the return of the trophy was jailed for two years.

This was the second stolen-trophy scandal, following the 1895 robbery of the original FA Cup when it was being exhibited in a Birmingham jeweller's window while held by Aston Villa. Many years later a man confessed that the silver trophy had been melted down and converted into hundreds of half-crown coins. Just think, the loose change in people's pockets could once have been held aloft in triumph by a winning captain.

After Pickles had played the hero the FA at last learned their lesson, and secretly had a copy of the World Cup made. All those films and photographs you see of the likes of Bobby Moore and Nobby Stiles holding the trophy aloft have one thing in common: it is *not* the real Jules Rimet Trophy, but a replica that is now on show at the National Football Museum in Preston.

The original Jules Rimet Trophy was won outright in 1970 by three-time winners Brazil, but they managed to have it stolen in 1983. This time there was no Pickles to sniff it out, and it has never been recovered.

The major trophies are now used only for the presentation ceremonies before being quickly replaced by duplicates. Nobody will confirm it, but you can take it from me that includes the Rugby World Cup that was paraded through London following England's triumph in 2003.

Before I get on with the Football World Cup funny stuff, here's a chilling fact: the first captain to lead out a World Cup team was later lined up against a wall and shot. French skipper Alex Villaplane proudly led his team out against Mexico for the first World Cup match on the Sunday afternoon of 13 July 1930, the day before Bastille Day. 'It is the proudest moment of my life,' he told reporters after leading France to a thumping 4–1 victory. Fifteen years later he was shot by French resistance fighters for allegedly collaborating with the Nazis during the Second World War.

But that's enough of the grim face of football. My objective in this book is to make you grin, so here are a few crackers that won't give you the World Cup willies.

The United States trainer raced on to the pitch to treat a player and protest to the referee over a disputed decision during the 1930 semi-final against Argentina. He stumbled and dropped his medical box and a bottle of chloroform smashed on the pitch. The trainer took the fumes full in the face, folded slowly to the ground like a puppet that had had its strings cut away and had to be carried back to the touchline by his players! He was the first World Cup wally.

Romania's entry in the 1930 World Cup finals gave a whole new meaning to 'By Royal Appointment'. King Carol II, known as the 'Playboy King', insisted that a representative team be sent to the tournament after the original invitation had been turned down because the players could not get the necessary two months off work. The King selected the team himself and then arranged time off on full pay for each of the players. They were eliminated from the competition after playing just two matches. When King Carol was overthrown in 1940, he fled to South America, where he was warmly remembered as the 'football-mad king'. In Romania, like our George III, he was just remembered as 'mad'.

Brazilian referee Almeida Rego caused a near riot by getting his timing wrong when France played Argentina in 1930. France were pressing for an equaliser when Señor Rego blew the final whistle just as French left-winger Marcel Langiller was shaping to shoot at the end of a fifty-yard run. Hundreds of Argentinian fans came dashing on to the pitch to celebrate their team's victory. While all this was going on, Referee Rego was being surrounded by French officials arguing that he had blown the whistle six minutes too early, and with Langiller poised to score. Rego's linesmen confirmed the clock-watching complaints, so the embarrassed referee had to order mounted police to clear the pitch. He instructed the teams to come back from the dressing-rooms, where several players were already in the bath. Argentinian inside-forward Roberto Ciero fainted when he was told he had to return to the pitch.

It took police and armed guards nearly half an hour to clear the playing area, and then the two teams played out the last six minutes without further score. The French wanted to clock the referee.

Perhaps the cliché 'a game of two halves' was first uttered when plans were being finalised for the first World Cup final on 30 July 1930. The organisers could not decide whether to play with a ball manufactured in Uruguay or one made in Argentina. So they played with both!

Argentina led 1–2 at the end of the first half, having played with their ball. Belgian referee Langenus, resplendent in knickerbockers, came out for the second half carrying a Uruguayan ball, and the host country went on to win 4–2. Centre-forward Hector Castro, who clinched victory with a last-minute goal, had only one hand, having lost part of an arm in a childhood accident.

Two boatloads of Argentinian fans crossing the River Plate to see the game were delayed by fog. They arrived just in time to see Uruguay parading the Jules Rimet Trophy around the pitch. They felt very fogged off. Or, something like that.

The Italians won the second World Cup final, staged in their home country. In the final, held in Rome on 10 June 1934, they beat Czechoslovakia 2–1 after extra-time, and after being a goal down in the seventieth minute. Raimundo Orsi, one of three South Americans in the Italian team, equalised with an astonishing curling shot, and Angelo Schiavio snatched the winner in the ninety-seventh minute of an exciting, evenly fought match. Fascist dictator Benito Mussolini presented the trophy to Italian captain and goalkeeper Giampiero Combi.

The day after the final, Orsi tried more than twenty times to repeat his big bender for the benefit of a posse of photographers. He failed every time.

Swiss centre-forward Poldi Kielholz, scorer of three goals in the 1934 finals, wore spectacles. So I was not a fashion trendsetter when I wore my bins while playing.

Leonidas da Silva, flamboyant star of the Brazilian attack, was unhappy playing against Poland on the muddy Strasbourg pitch in the 1938 finals. He decided he would have better footing if he went back to his boyhood days, when he played barefooted. But the moment he removed his boots and tossed them nonchalantly over the touchline, the referee ordered him to put them back on because it was in contravention of the laws of the game to play without boots. Nike and Puma breathed huge sighs of relief.

Leonidas, 'the Black Diamond' and the Pele of his day, then became sure-footed enough to score four goals in Brazil's 6–5 victory. Ernest Wilimowski scored four goals for Poland before finishing on the losing side. He said afterwards, *'A jestem chore jak poniewa.'* (Which, I am assured, translates as 'I am as sick as a parrot.')

Italian skipper Peppino Meazza had that sinking feeling as he scored the semi-final penalty against Brazil that clinched a place in the 1938 final for the World Cup holders. As he steered the spot-kick into the net his shorts, torn earlier in the game, slipped down to leave him exposed. His celebrating team-mates hid his blushes until a new pair were produced.

Hungarian goalkeeper Antal Szabo startled visitors to the dressing-room after Hungary's 4–2 defeat against Italy in the final in Paris on 19 June 1938. He told them, 'I have never felt so proud in my life.' As his audience looked on dumbstruck, he explained, 'We may have lost the match but we have saved eleven lives. The Italian players received a telegram from Mussolini before the game that read, "Win or die!" Now they can go home as heroes.'

With war clouds gathering over Europe in 1939, FIFA president Jules Rimet reclaimed from the Italian FA the trophy that bore his name. He thought long and hard about where it would be safest, and – with French logic – finally decided that the only place was the bedroom. For the duration of the Second World War the Jules Rimet Trophy nestled under his bed as football – as it had been in 1914 – was once again interrupted by shooting of the unacceptable kind.

England's squad for the 1950 finals trained by running around Ascot racecourse before leaving for Brazil. Unfortunately, they finished as also-rans. The thoroughbreds were beaten by the American carthorses.

It was more like a war than a football match when Hungary and Brazil clashed in the 1954 quarter-finals in Berne. The game was continually spilling over with violence, and British referee Arthur Ellis had to have a police escort from the pitch after ordering off three players. The fighting continued in the dressing-rooms after Hungary had won 4–2, and players from both sides were cut and gashed by broken bottles. 'The Brazilians accused me of being a communist and I was spat at,' said Ellis. 'It was the most difficult match I ever handled, and I could easily have sent six players off from each side.'

Arthur's match fee for being the man in the middle of a war? Just four pounds! It would not even have bought him his whistle for *It's a Knockout!*

Hungary's long unbeaten record of twenty-nine games (including historic 6–3 and 7–1 victories over England) finally crashed at the heartbreak hurdle of the 1954 World Cup final. Puskas, less than 100 per cent fit, scored one goal and had another perfectly good-looking one ruled offside by English referee Bill Ling. It was the unheralded West Germans, featuring the Walter brothers, Fritz and Otmar – both wartime paratroopers – who became the new champions with a 3–2 victory.

But that Hungarian team of the early 1950s will always be remembered by anybody from my generation as one of the greatest combinations ever to operate on a football pitch. After they'd put those thirteen goals past England goalkeeper Gil Merrick in two matches, when he came to Liverpool to play for Birmingham City we used to shout, 'Watch out, Puskas is about.' It always gave him the jitters.

Both England and Scotland were sent packing by Uruguay in the 1954 finals. The Scots, beaten 1–0 by Austria in their World Cup finals debut, were then destroyed 7–0 by the Uruguayans in a match played in a heatwave. 'We were given such a chasing that we came off at the final whistle with sunburned tongues,' said the always-good-for-a-laugh Tommy Docherty.

It was not quite so funny for team manager Andy Beattie. He got so fed up with interference from the amateur Scottish selectors that he walked out on the job after just one game!

The 1954 quarter-final between Austria and host nation Switzerland produced one of the most remarkable of all World Cup matches. The Austrians were 0–3 down after twenty-three minutes. Ten minutes later they were leading 5–3. By half-time the score was 5–4, and Austria had missed a penalty. They finally won 7–5, with all twelve goals coming in the space of just forty-nine minutes of playing time. Apparently, the Swiss rolled over.

Northern Ireland brought humour as well as skill and endeavour to the 1958 finals in Sweden. As they marched through to the quarter-finals, skipper Danny 'Blarney King' Blanchflower told startled reporters, 'Our secret tactic is to equalise before the opposition scores.'

Told that their opponents had been tucked up in bed hours earlier, manager Peter Doherty (he could play a bit!) broke off from a game of near-midnight cards with his players to respond, 'Maybe they did go to bed hours ago. But are they sleeping?'

The Irish had a party after every match during the finals, win, lose or draw. A foreign journalist walked into a swinging party after they had been soundly beaten 3–1 by Argentina. 'What on earth have you got to celebrate?' he asked Doherty.

'We're drowning our sorrows,' the manager said with a grin.

Now we know who Mike Bassett modelled himself on.

Pele – out injured in the 1962 finals – was so pleased and delighted with the two-goal debut of his deputy Amarildo for Brazil against Spain that he jumped fully clothed into the team bath after the match to congratulate him.

A special 1966 World Cup stamp – approved by the Post Office – featured the flags of the sixteen finalists. They were all set to run off the presses in their millions when the Foreign Office objected because the government did not recognise North Korea. So they quickly rushed out alternatives showing footballers, which became the first British stamps to feature sportsmen. Now that takes some licking.

You're nicked! It looks as if German referee Rudolf Kreitlein has been arrested, but he is actually being given police protection to save him from Argentinian players. They were going nuts over his decision to send off their skipper Antonio Rattin during the 1966 World Cup quarter-final against England at Wembley. That's referee supremo Ken Aston with a hand on his shoulder. Rattin wanted to put his hands around Kreitlein's neck!

Those of us who were around in 1966 will never ever forget the quarter-final between England and Argentina. Blimey, I thought it was going to trigger the Third World War. In a bitterly fought match, England just about got the better of a talented but temperamental Argentinian side. It was real argy-bargy stuff after their wonderfully skilful skipper Antonio Rattin had been ordered off because of his contemptuous attitude towards the ref. West German referee Rudolf Kreitlein explained, 'I sent him off because of a look in his eyes. I did not need to speak his language. The look on his face was enough to show that he thought he was in charge of things. Only one of us could referee the game, and it was not going to be him. His arrogance and defiance caused great disruption.'

It took the English head of the referees' panel, Ken Aston, working with interpreters on the touchline, ten minutes to restore order as the entire Argentinian team threatened to walk off. Rattin, one of the best players in the tournament, took eight minutes to saunter around the perimeter of the pitch and to the dressing-rooms, leaving chaos and confusion in his wake. There has rarely been such a commotion in a game of this importance.

The Argentinians saw it as a European plot, and embassies were attacked back in Buenos Aires. Geoff Hurst headed the only goal of the game. To have made it *really* controversial perhaps he should have knocked the ball in with his hand. But who could possibly get away with *that* in a World Cup?

Jack Charlton was given an unusual memento of the 1966 World Cup finals – a kiddie's potty. Two players were selected at random after each game to give a urine sample, and Big Jack got chosen every time for the dope test. His team-mates dubbed him the 'Jimmy Riddle champion' and presented the potty to him at a mock awards ceremony. Jack said, 'You must be taking the piss!'

To this day, the Germans dispute Geoff Hurst's second goal in extra-time of the 1966 final. Tireless Alan Ball tore down the right, and his centre found Hurst, who spun round and crashed a shot against the underside of the bar. As the ball bounced down, Roger Hunt – the England player closest to the net – immediately whirled round in celebration of a goal. Hunt's opinion was supported by Russian linesman Tofik Bakhramov, who signalled with a vigorous nod of the head that the ball had crossed the line. The Germans blamed his decision on the war!

All I will say is that I watched Roger Hunt play many times for Liverpool and he was the most honest footballer you could wish to clap eyes on. If he reckoned the ball was over the line – and he was the nearest to it – then that's good enough for me.

When I was sniffing around for World Cup stories, I was told this cracker that has the unlikely pairing of Alf Ramsey and Henry Cooper: Sir Alf left the FA, for whom he had made millions, with a paltry £6500 pay-off in 1974. Later in the year a British Trade Salutes Alf Ramsey testimonial dinner was staged at London's Café Royal. Prime Minister Harold Wilson was chief speaker, and he said that the World Cup had saved his bacon. The economy was so bad that during the summer of 1966 there was a threat of devaluation of the pound, but the great British public hardly noticed it because their minds were concentrated on England's run to the final.

An extraordinary thing happened while the Prime Minister was paying his tribute to Sir Alf. A mouse ran the length of the top table until Henry Cooper put out his famous left hand and caught it. He handed it to a member of the staff, who stamped on it. All of this brought roars from the audience, first of laughter and then of anguish as the mouse came to its unfortunate end. The Prime Minister thought it was a reaction to his speech!

Mr Wilson was followed by football writer *par excellence* Geoffrey Green, who was peerless as an after-dinner speaker. He took out a mouth organ and started to play 'Moon River'. 'Alf, old boy,' he said, 'this is to get you in the mood for your new career. Let's go out busking.'

And here's another cracking story passed on to me about Geoffrey Green. England skipper Bobby Moore was arrested on a trumped-up jewel-theft charge while in Colombia on the eve of the 1970 World Cup finals. When he arrived in Mexico to rejoin the England squad after four days under arrest, a posse of press photographers and reporters were waiting on the tarmac at Mexico City airport as his plane from Bogota touched down. Among them was the unique Geoffrey, Corinthian football correspondent of *The Times*. He had a habit of using lyrics when he talked, and he always greeted people with phrases like 'Younger than springtime . . .' or 'Over the rainbow, baby . . .' This in a cut-glass Oxbridge accent. In fact, the intellectual Geoffrey was the first person heard to say 'I'm over the moon', long before it became the cliché crutch of tongue-tied footballers.

As Bobby stepped out from the plane to be met by dazzling flash-bulbs, he spotted the tall, willowy figure of Peter O'Toole-lookalike Geoffrey among the hordes at the bottom of the plane steps. Bobby punched a fist into the air and shouted, 'Over the rainbow, baby!' Foreign reporters, anxious to record Bobby's first words on his return to freedom, scratched their heads as they tried to decipher what the England captain had said.

The next day Jimmy Greaves arrived in Mexico City in a battered Ford Escort at the end of the *Daily Mirror*-sponsored 16,400-mile London-to-Mexico World Cup Rally in which he and his co-driver Tony Fall finished a creditable sixth. Jimmy's main concern as he climbed out of his car was for his West Ham team-mate and best pal Bobby. 'Mooro wouldn't take a liberty, let alone a bracelet,' he said.

He found out that Moore was hiding out at the home of a British embassy official, who was keeping him out of sight of the press pack. Jimmy climbed over the back wall surrounding the garden and disappeared from view. Several hours – and quite a few lagers – later he described how he had been caught by the embassy official's wife, given a bollocking and then allowed in to see Bobby. Jimmy's first words were, 'Show us the bracelet then, Mooro.'

The embassy official's wife overheard and went ashen faced. When it came to humour, she and Greavsie were from different planets.

After Brazil had beaten Italy 4–1 in one of the best World Cup finals in Mexico in 1970, the Brazilian players were engulfed in a tidal wave of fans, many of them photographers and radio interviewers wanting to celebrate rather than capture the moment. An impromptu Mardi Gras carnival had suddenly broken out on the Azteca pitch. Rivelino collapsed under the weight of the celebrations and had to be carried to the dressing-room on a stretcher.

The huge mob was still waiting for Carlos Alberto and his team-mates after they had battled through to the awards ceremony. The Brazilian skipper did not notice as he paraded the Jules Rimet Trophy that a gold attachment to the cup had fallen to the ground. Brazilian reserve Dario retrieved it just as a young spectator was making for the exit with his unexpected souvenir.

Tostao, Pele's plundering partner in attack, refused to swap his shirt with any Italian player. He had promised to give it to the surgeon in Houston, Texas, who had performed two operations on a detached retina the previous year. Five years later, Tostao himself qualified as a medical doctor.

The Germans staged a spectacular opening ceremony to the 1974 finals that showcased their meticulous planning and organisation, but they overlooked one minor detail (just like they forgot it snowed in Russia during the winter). As Brazil and Yugoslavia lined up for the kick-off to the opening match in Frankfurt the referee delayed the start while embarrassed officials hustled around the pitch inserting the corner and centre-line flags.

The 1974 final between West Germany and Holland in Munich got off to an extraordinary start when English referee Jack Taylor, a master butcher from Wolverhampton, awarded a penalty in the first minute. From the kick-off, Holland played a stunning series of fifteen passes before Johan Cruyff made a dash for goal. He was tripped by Uli Hoeness, and Taylor had no hesitation in pointing to the spot.

Neeskens put away the penalty, but just as it looked as if West Germany were going to be paralysed by the strolling players of Holland they got back into the game thanks to a second penalty awarded by Taylor. This time Paul Breitner, an artist of a left-back who was a highly intelligent and politically motivated Maoist, scored from the spot to make it 1–1. The Germans then took command and ace opportunist Gerd Müller swept the ball into the net for his sixty-eighth international goal and the winner for the host country.

Franz Beckenbauer, the imperious *Kaiser* of the German team, said, 'It was a brave decision by the referee to give that penalty so early in the match, but I instinctively felt that we too would get a penalty at some stage.'

'Johnston is the first disgrace of the World Cup,' screamed Argentinian newspaper headlines after Scotland's Willie Johnston tested positive for drug-taking at the 1978 tournament. (Willie protested his innocence and claimed he had been taking tablets to beat the 'flu). Back home, Scotland's desperate draw with Iran was considered a bigger disgrace, and the television directors had a ball focusing on manager Ally Macleod having a nervous breakdown on the touchline bench. But he brought it upon himself by suggesting that Scotland would win the World Cup. Win it my arse.

The 1978 final, in which Argentina beat Holland 3–1 after extra-time, was always bordering on the vicious, and the referee awarded fifty free-kicks. Eerily, the front row of the main stand was one long line of Argentinian generals. This was not the sort of image that FIFA wanted to portray for the Beautiful Game.

The bad feeling between the two sides erupted even before a ball was kicked in the final. Holland threatened a walk-off protest when Argentina captain Daniel Passarella objected to Italian referee Sergio Gonella about a small plaster cast on Rene Van der Kerkhof's hand, which was protecting a bruised bone. Passarella claimed the cast was dangerous. Spanish-speaking Dutch midfielder Johan Neeskens told the Argentine captain, 'If Rene goes, we all go.' Gonella finally persuaded Van der Kerkhof to return to the dressing-room to have soft bandaging put on his injury and delayed the kick-off until his return, much to the hair-tearing frustration of deadline-dictated TV directors around the globe.

Italy were the winners in Spain in 1982 with a Jekyll-and-Hyde performance. They were cautious and cynical in the first three matches as they concentrated purely on qualifying for the later rounds. Then they produced a flood of freestyle football to beat defending champions Argentina, tournament favourites Brazil, Poland (who finished third) and, in the final, European champions West Germany.

The tournament's top scorer with six goals was Paolo Rossi, restored to the Italian team after a ban for his alleged involvement in a bribery scandal had been lifted.

They were the silent champions. They went through the entire tournament without talking to the Italian press in protest at scathing criticism on the way to the finals. Blimey, I wish some of our players would treat us to some silence instead of their tedious bloody clichés.

Pals of mine who are lucky to have their asses always parked in press box seats have passed on many of the stories in this chapter, including this one about a marvellous bit of French farce during the 1982 World Cup match between France and Kuwait.

Following a disallowed goal, it looked to everybody who saw it as if the all-powerful Kuwaiti FA president – a prince – was calling his players off in protest. The referee altered his decision and peace was restored. Later, it was denied that the prince had been signalling his players to come off, with it being claimed that he was ordering them to stay on. An incredulous journalist at the press conference said, 'I know you read right to left, so are we now to believe that this gesture [he beckoned towards himself] means to stay where you are?' There were no more questions. Everybody was laughing too much.

Argentina, of course, won the 'Hand of God' finals in Mexico in 1986. It might have been a different story had Brazil arrived for the finals with a full-strength team. Renato Gaucho, their wayward genius of a winger, was notorious for liking the nightlife, and he was kicked out of the squad for breaking a curfew at the training camp just prior to leaving for Mexico. His Flamengo clubmate Leandro, one of the world's finest defenders at the time, pulled out in protest, so Brazil arrived in Mexico understrength and under stress.

Questions were asked in Parliament when television cameras picked up a banner being held proudly aloft by half a dozen sozzled-looking English fans on the terraces in Mexico during the 1986 finals. It read, 'Scousers on the dole drinking tequila.'

Who can ever forget the tears on the face of the clown – Paul Gascoigne, of course – during the epic 1990 World Cup semi-final against Germany? Young Gazza, who had been more productive and prominent in midfield than German skipper Lothar Matthäus, collected a second booking of the tournament in extra-time. He knew this would rule him out of the final, and he could not stop the tears rolling down his face as the game finished at 1–1 and went to penalties.

Terry 'El Tel' Venables, manager of the World XI for a 1987 charity match, tells Diego Maradona: 'Remember, Diego, this is a game of football not *hand*ball.'

The Germans converted all their spot-kicks against outstanding goalkeeper Peter Shilton, while Stuart Pearce and Chris Waddle failed for England ... and would later be rewarded for their incompetence with lucrative pizza-plugging TV commercials in which they took the mickey out of themselves. I think they were taking the pizza out of all of us.

In 1990 West Germany beat Argentina 1–0 in a best-forgotten repeat of the 1986 final, memorable only because it made Franz Beckenbauer the first man to captain and manage a World Cup-winning team. It was a snarling, spoiling match settled in the eighty-fifth minute by an Andreas Brehme spot-kick. The Argentinians angrily claimed the penalty should not have been awarded following what looked like a piece of theatrics by Rudi Völler, who was almost in the Jürgen Klinsmann class as an ace diver. They should have rewarded them with high-tariff marks instead of Deutschmarks.

It was an appalling performance by Argentina, who had Maradona whingeing throughout, and they finished with nine men. Pedro Monzon became the first player ever dismissed in a World Cup final in the sixty-fourth minute for a reckless tackle. In the closing stages, with tempers out of control and Mexican referee Edgardo Mendez out of his depth, Gustavo Dezotti was shown the red card after wrestling German defender Jürgen Kohler to the ground. The Beautiful Game? No, this shamed football.

For World Cup '94 nobody was quite sure how the Americans would react to the 'soccer' finals being played throughout the United States. ('Soccer is a Kick in the Grass' was one of their clever selling lines.) The Americans supported the matches in record numbers (3,587,538 spectators in total), and deserved much better than the dreary final between Brazil and Italy that was, disgracefully, decided on penalties rather than with a replay. It somehow cheapened the greatest football show on earth. Brazil emerged winners after Italian idol Roberto 'the Divine Ponytail' Baggio had fired his penalty high over the bar in the sad shoot-out in Los Angeles.

I would like to have seen Baggio take a penalty against our own Divine Ponytail David Seaman. That would have been quite hair-raising.

Who was the first person to miss a penalty in the 1994 finals? The answer is Miss Diana Ross, who in the opening ceremony in Chicago had to kick the ball into an empty net from all of three yards. She missed by five feet, but the rehearsed collapse of the goal still worked! It was not Diana's supreme moment.

Miracle-worker Jack Charlton – surely worthy of being called O'Charlton – once again motivated the Republic of Ireland team beyond expectations in the 1994 finals, and they got through to the second round before being eliminated by Holland. Big Jack was involved in a touchline row with officials for tossing bottles of water to his players to try to combat the threat of dehydration during games played under the scorching midday sun to satisfy European television schedules. I would have given him a knighthood for caring about his team.

The 1994 quarter-final between Mexico and Bulgaria was held up when the Mexican goal collapsed under the weight of several players falling into the net. As groundsmen trundled a new goal on to the pitch, a commentator said, 'This substitute will be better than the original.' He was known as a net prophet.

During the build-up to the 1998 finals we got wind that all was not well in the England camp. It was all over the back pages that the media were concerned about the way Glenn Hoddle was managing affairs. My feeling from my spectator's seat was that, for a man who had been a creative conductor of a player, he was strangely cautious and indecisive when wearing his England manager's hat. He seemed set to disappear in a maze of his own making, and had oddball things going on such as consulting his faith healer Eileen Drewery and encouraging his players to go to see her.

He had also secretly entered into an agreement to write his diary of World Cup events in harness with FA spokesman David Davies, while telling only half the story at tense press conferences. He had an enormous bust-up with Paul Gascoigne when dropping him from the squad at the last minute, but the facts came out only in drips to a press pack desperate for news. The media got behind Hoddle and his team for the finals in France, but if anything were to go wrong they were ready to drop on 'Hod the God' with the weight of the lead off a church roof. Now you know why he had little or no support from

Fleet Street when he made his stupid remark about disabled people paying for the sins of earlier lives, a crass comment that cost him his job.

I loved the story that circulated when the Eileen Drewery, um, witch-hunt was at its peak. Apparently, Hoddle once ordered all the players carrying niggling injuries to sit on a row of chairs. Eileen Drewery then passed along the back of the row, placing her hands on the top of each player's head, asking what their injury was and transferring 'power' to the healing process. When she got to Ray Parlour and placed her hands on his head he is alleged to have said, 'Short back and sides, please', and burst out laughing. Hoddle was said to have blown a gasket and sent him home. It was a Parlour game too far.

The 1998 World Cup final was a strange affair. Brazil were roasting-hot favourites to beat host nation France and retain their championship, but only one team turned up on the day. France, with two-goal Zinedine Zidane in imperious form, virtually cantered to a 3–0 victory.

At the after-match inquest into Brazil's punchless performance it emerged that the gifted Ronaldo – the 'new Pele' – had suffered some sort of fit and had been given tranquillisers. He played like a man in a trance, and his team-mates did not seem to be able to get out of second gear. Brazil denied the story that Ronaldo had played only because of pressure put on them by their kit sponsors. Football was now in the throttling hands of the commercial companies. Mike Bassett would like to get *them* by their throats.

England skipper David Beckham was less than 100 per cent fit going into the 2002 finals after breaking a bone in his foot in the service of Manchester United. Suddenly 'metatarsal' was part of everyday conversation as the Beckham foot became a focal point of attention. It developed into much more than just a footnote when Becks, as the tabloid headline writers had dubbed him, recovered in time to score the penalty that sank Argentina in a group match. That finally put to rest the ghosts that had haunted him for four years since his sending-off against the same team at France '98.

Brazil, gifted their 2–1 victory over England, went on to win the World Cup for a fifth time, with the revived Ronaldo scoring both goals in a 2–0 victory over Germany to make up for his virtual non-appearance in the 1998 final in Paris.

The Republic of Ireland were the talk of the 2002 tournament for all the wrong reasons. Skipper Roy Keane, arguably the most influential midfield player of the decade, was sent home after a vicious verbal attack on team manager Mick McCarthy just before the tournament was scheduled to start. This page would have to be printed on asbestos for me to publish verbatim what Keane shouted at McCarthy during their face-to-face bust-up. By all accounts it included twenty f—s, a lot of b—s, a couple of c—s, and two wankers.

Even without their main player, the Irish battled through to the knockout stage before going out on penalties to Spain.

Brian Clough had been Roy Keane's first manager in his Nottingham Forest days. Asked if he would have sent the Irishman home following his row with McCarthy, Cloughie said, 'Yes, I would certainly have sent him home . . . But first of all I would have shot him.'

Trevor Sinclair helped England beat Argentina in Sapporo in the 2002 finals, and was then selected for the after-match dope test. He was in a hurry to join his celebrating team-mates and dashed on to the coach outside the dressing-room, looked around and was fairly disturbed to find that he was sitting with the Argentinians. He had climbed aboard the wrong coach.

Finally from the World Cup front, the following media-apology communiqué brought light relief to the tense 2002 finals:

The BBC has apologised to deaf football fans after its World Cup subtitle service turned live text commentary on screen into gobbledegook. Viewers who followed the subtitles on Ceefax during Portugal's 2002 World Cup clash with Poland found the East European country renamed Holland, while the ball became a boule.

Scots referee Hugh Dallas was re-christened Huge Dallas Texas, while the Portuguese striker João Pinto played as So Pointed and Liverpool and Poland keeper Jerzy Dudek was billed as Jersey Dud Cheque. Portuguese defender Costa appeared as Cost a Lot, Luis Figo as Loose Fig and midfielder Pedro Barbosa as Petrol Barbarian. Face Porthole should have read FC Porto, and the game was played in Jeonju, Korea, not Joan's Jujitsu Career. A viewer who called in to complain said, 'It read like a script from a Monty Python sketch.'

A BBC spokesman blamed the fault on the speech-recognition machine, which is programmed to translate the voice of a commentator into text within seconds. The machine confused words it was not used to, particularly foreign names, with other names and words.

'Some machines have mistaken the odd word,' the spokesman explained, 'and this caused a few problems during the Portugal–Poland match. We apologise to any viewers who experienced any difficulty reading the text.'

But for Poland it was more entertaining than the game. They were thumped 4–0. Or, as Ceefax put it: Porthole 4, Holland 0.

It's enough to give you the World Cup willies!

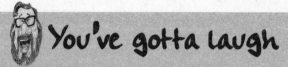

You've gotta laugh

It was the World Cup final at Wembley in 1966, and there was not a ticket to be had. A spectator squashed on the terraces noticed an empty seat just in front of the Royal Box, so he dodged the stewards and managed to make his way there while all eyes were on the match.

'All right if I sit here, pal?' he says to the man sitting in the next seat.

'It's empty,' he replies. 'You're welcome to sit there.'

'I can't believe I've found an empty seat. Who in their right mind would miss a game of this historic importance?'

'It was my wife's seat,' the neighbouring man explains. 'Sadly she passed away and so for the first time since our marriage forty years ago I have come to a Wembley game on my own. We always used to come together.'

'How sad,' says the man now settling comfortably into his unexpected seat. 'But I'm surprised you could not have found a friend or relative to come with you.'

'I did offer,' says his neighbour, 'but they all preferred to go to the funeral.'

Hark who's talking

Peter Shilton:
'You've got to believe that you're going to win, and I believe we'll win the World Cup until the final whistle blows and we're knocked out.'

Nick Hancock:
'If David Seaman's dad had worn a condom, we'd still be in the World Cup.'

David Beckham (According to an expert lip-reader after Ronaldinho's free-kick goal against David Seaman in the 2002 World Cup finals):
'Not your fault, mate, that he fluked the f***er in.'

Sammy McIlroy:
'I am manager of Macclesfield and am giving the job my total commitment. Obviously, as an Irishman, I want the job as Ireland's international manager.'

Craig Brown:
'I strongly feel that the only difference between the two teams were the goals that England scored.'

Graham Taylor:
'Very few of us have any idea whatsoever of what life is like living in a goldfish bowl – except, of course, for those of us who are goldfish.'

Tommy Docherty:
'The ball spent so much time in the air that we didn't need a referee and two linesmen. We needed Air Traffic Control at Heathrow.'

Bruce Rioch:
'We threw our dice into the ring and turned up trumps.'

Mike Walker:
'I just wonder what would have happened if the shirt had been on the other foot.'

Bob Paisley:
'Yes, I have to admit we've had some bad times at Anfield. One year, I remember, we came second.'

Sir Alf Ramsey:
'I gave the players strict instructions not to swap shirts with the Argentinians. I did not want animals having England shirts.'

Sir Bobby Robson:
'I do want to play the long ball, and I do want to play the short ball. I think long and short balls is what the game is all about.'

Dave Bassett:
'And I honestly believe we can go all the way to Wembley – unless somebody knocks us out.'

Dick Graham:
'I wouldn't dream of criticising Jack Charlton, but he was the weak link.'

George Graham:
'Nigel Winterburn was caught as immobile as a moving lamppost.'

Gary Megson:
'The only bad thing about our situation is the situation itself.'

Ken Brown:
'With our luck, one of our players must be bonking a witch.'

10 The Supporting Cast

I could easily go into a Mike Bassett rant about the way football fans are treated by the high and mighty clubs. Supporters are the lifeblood of the game, but in recent years they have had the blood sucked from them by clubs so greedy for their money that they are like backstreet muggers. Bloody hell, you could feed and clothe a family on what it costs just one fan to follow his team for a season.

This book is aimed to make you laugh, and I apologise for bringing a mood of gloom and doom into its pages, but I feel so strongly about the issue of overcharging that I will use any platform I can to shout and scream about the galloping greed that is eating into the very fabric of football. Excuse the all-our-yesterdays tone, but when I was a nipper my dad used to take me on the Kop and buy me a pie without feeling as if he'd had to work all week for the privilege of us watching the Reds.

How about this, just to show I can come up with constructive comments rather than just a loud-mouthed tirade: bring back the maximum wage! When I was a youngster players were on what were called 'soccer-slave' wages of twenty pounds a week. They were the bad old days, but how about pinning the top wage at twenty thousand a week. Blimey, 99.9 per cent people in the land will never get to sniff earnings like that. This would stop the crazy situation we have of many players taking more than fifty grand a week from the game. Much of that money comes out of the pockets of the fans. If the clubs could get their wage bills down to sensible levels, they could pass the savings on to the fans by charging a lot less to watch what is, in many cases, pretty dull and dire football.

OK, that's the soapbox stuff over. Now on with the fun. This chapter is all about the fanatics who support their clubs through thick, thin and thorny times. There are few, if any, more football-mad cities than mine. You are either red- or blue-blooded, Anfield or Goodison, and there is no crossing the line (with the possible exception of my mam, of course).

Here's a Tomlinson theory: I don't think the wit of football fans is as quick and sharp as it was when they were all standing. Thinking on our feet was easy, particularly when crowded into the Kop. It was like being on stage at the Liverpool Empire. It was bloody hilarious, but now they are on their bums, their brains have gone numb in comparison with the comedians who graced (and sometimes *dis*graced) the Kop when I was in the springtime of my footie watching.

A supporter new to the Kop in the days when we were a steaming, perspiring standing mountain of red-blooded men turned to the bloke behind him and said, 'Look at that dirty bugger. He's just pissed in the pocket of the feller in front.'

'Stop moaning,' said the bloke behind. 'You didn't complain when I pissed in *your* pocket.'

One of the most famous and best-remembered examples of Scouse humour came when Ian St John was an idol at Anfield. A poster outside a Liverpool church read, 'What will you do when Jesus returns among us?' A graffiti reply read, 'Switch St John to inside-left.'

Alan Ball found out about the fanaticism of the Merseyside fans when he joined Everton. One day he was leaving Goodison Park in a hurry after a match to join the England squad. He was carrying a suitcase in one hand and a hold-all in the other when he was confronted by an Everton supporter.

''Ere, Al pal, gi's yer autograph,' he said in thick Scouse as he held a blank piece of paper under Ballie's nose.

'Can't you see I've got my hands full?' said Alan, desperate to catch a train.

'Don't worry, pal,' said the fan. 'Just spit on the paper. That'll do me.'

Alec Stock used to tell a story that captures the intense rivalry between Liverpool and Everton supporters:

When I was manager of Fulham, we were drawn to play Everton in the FA Cup. On the day of the match I went ahead to Goodison with our coach Bill Taylor. We had our wicker skips with us containing all our kit, and we caught a taxi to the ground. Our cabbie recognised me and quickly declared that he was a rabid Liverpool supporter.

'I'll be on me knees praying fer yer,' he told me. 'I'll ask Him upstairs to let Fulham give Everton the hiding of their lives.'

He pulled up outside the main entrance to Goodison and just sat there while Bill and I struggled to get the skips on to the pavement.

'I don't suppose there's any chance of you helping us carry this kit through to the dressing-rooms?' I asked him, trying not to sound sarcastic.

'Sorry, Mr Stock,' he said. 'I get paralysed as soon as I get within smelling distance of this place. I wouldn't go in there if you offered me fifty quid. Just make sure you effing-well hammer them.'

With that he drove off, leaving Bill and me laughing our heads off as we handled the gear by ourselves. As it happened, we won in the big upset of the round. That would have been better than a tip to the cabbie.

I know I'm biased, but it's still hard to beat the wit of the Scouse fans, even though they're not quite in the same league as the Kopites of the fifties and sixties. I was at Anfield for a League game once when it started snowing. The Kop choir quickly filled the ground with choruses of 'Jingle Bells' followed by 'The First Noël'. It was the middle of March.

Another time it hissed down during a European Cup night, and the pitch became so flooded that the game had to be abandoned. 'Send out the lifeboats,' came the shout from the terraces. 'Shanks will be all right. He can walk across the pitch.'

And I was there when a blanket of fog dropped on Anfield while Liverpool were playing Walsall in an FA Cup tie. Standing on the Kop, we could just about see a shadowy figure shoot the ball into the net at the Anfield Road End.

As one, we chanted, 'Who scored the goal? Who scored the goal?'

From the Anfield Road End came the chorused reply, 'Tony Hateley scored. Tony Hateley scored.'

The Kop choir responded immediately to the tune of 'Aintree Iron', 'Thank you very much for the information, thank you very, very much.'

Ah, football fans. Who can touch them for inventive and innovative comedy? Here are some more examples.

Malcolm Finlayson, one of the great Scottish goalkeepers, who followed Bert Williams as the last line of the Wolves defence, started his career with Millwall. 'The Millwall fans were in the Merseyside class for humour,' says Malcolm, who became a wealthy steel manufacturer after he hung up his gloves. 'I remember coming out on to the pitch after a losing first half at the time of the German War Crimes Tribunal. "They hanged the wrong bloody eleven at Nuremberg," one of our supporters shouted. I could hardly play for laughing.'

Anybody who knows their boxing will recall one of Muhammad Ali's most famous fights when he first changed his name from Cassius Clay. He had a bitter championship showdown contest with the human skyscraper Ernie Terrell, who refused to call him by his new name. Throughout the fight Ali taunted Terrell with the question, 'What's mah name?' A few days later Tottenham were playing Fulham at White Hart Lane when Spurs schemer Terry Venables and Fulham defender Fred Callaghan got involved in some fisticuffs that led to them both being ordered off. As they were sparring and threatening to throw punches at each other, a voice from the terraces pleaded, 'For f***'s sake, Fred, tell him your name.'

There surely can't be fans more fanatical than those who parade around pitches as their club mascot, dressed in outrageous costumes and clowning (and often crowing) to stoke up the crowd.

I wish I had been there to witness the vicious confrontation between Swansea's Cyril the Swan and Millwall's Zampa the Lion in 2001. You would have put money on the lion to win their rage war on the pitch, but it was the swan who came out on top. He pulled off the lion's head and drop-kicked it into the crowd!

Cyril the Swan was the 'Bites Yer Legs' Hunter of mascots. He got himself in trouble for throwing rubbish at fans, disrupted a lottery draw and was banned for two matches after an altercation with Norwich City director of football Brian Hamilton.

The seven-foot-tall bird once ran on to the pitch and put a wing around a goalscorer in celebration, and got himself fined a thousand pounds by the Welsh FA for invading the field of play. That should have been his swansong.

Wolfie, the Wolverhampton Wanderers mascot, got involved in an on-pitch battle with the Three Little Pigs, who were advertising a double-glazing firm during a match against Bristol City at Ashton Gate. The wolf was huffing and puffing but was being held at bay by the pigs until City Cat – representing Bristol – came diving in and knocked the pigs for six. The referee didn't know whether to report the incident to the FA or the RSPCA.

For the cat, it was a welcome return to the spotlight. While making his debut two years earlier he had run around the pitch waving to the fans when his shorts came down. That let the cat out of the bag.

QPR mascot Jude the Cat was devastated when the referee ordered him away from the touchline because he was being mistaken for a player. 'How can I be mistaken for a player, for goodness' sake,' miaowed Jude. 'I'm a seven-foot black cat! I have an appeal in to the Football Association. This is a clear case of cat discrimination.'

That was really milking it.

The owner of a chippie close to Leeds United's Elland Road ground could not understand why his business was suddenly falling away. Then he realised what was wrong when a Leeds fan told him where he could stick his cutlery. He had ordered red knives and forks . . . and that made Leeds fans see the red of their hated rivals Manchester United. He changed to white plastic cutlery and the crisis was over. He also hid the tomato ketchup.

As a promotion at a chippie near Sunderland's Stadium of Light, the proprietor David Miller offered a free bag of chips to any supporter turning up in his club strip for their first visit to the shop. One fan arrived in his Sunderland strip, had his chips, then returned the next day in a Newcastle shirt and had a second helping. David Miller was furious. 'I didn't mind him having two bags of chips,' he said, 'but what self-respecting Sunderland fan would wear a Newcastle shirt?'

Frank Saul, who scored for Tottenham in the 1967 FA Cup final against Chelsea, wound down his career with Queen's Park Rangers, where, in one match, he was having a bit of a nightmare. During the second half and just after Saul had missed an open goal a dog came scampering on to the pitch. The game was held up while players and officials attempted to round up the intruder. The chase was still in progress when a loud Cockney voice boomed from the stand, 'Leave the dog on – take Saul off.'

It's amazing what football can do to even perfectly sane people. Delia Smith, the queen of the kitchen, has always conducted herself on screen with quiet dignity and seems a butter-wouldn't-melt-in-her-mouth type of demure lady. But the minute she puts on her Norwich City scarf – she is a director and chief benefactor of the club – she becomes a different person. Witness her amazing performance during half-time in a relegation battle with Manchester City at Carrow Road in the winter of 2005. She stood on the pitch with a microphone in her hand, and literally screamed at the Norwich supporters: 'Where are yer? Let's be 'avin' yer!' She was apparently trying to cook up a storm against the opposition, but her recipe failed and Norwich were beaten 2–3 after leading 2–0.

Delia later denied that she had been at the cooking sherry.

A new stand was built at Stamford Bridge when Brian Mears was Chelsea chairman. Shortly after it had been completed – and Chelsea had been soundly beaten in a home match – Mears received a letter from a disgruntled season-ticket holder that read, 'I would like to draw your attention to a major architectural design fault with the new stand. It's facing the pitch.'

Sir Bobby Robson told this story of his days managing at Ipswich, and it will be appreciated more if you take into account the deadly seriousness with which he has always approached training:

Graham Taylor is saying to Bobby Robson (left), 'Look at that plonker over there.' Robson replies, 'Yes, but he's not a turnip like you.' Taylor was dubbed 'the Turnip' and Robson 'the Plonker' during their up-and-down reigns as England managers.

The training ground at Ipswich was at the back of the main stand and very open to the public. During school holidays there was always an audience for our training sessions, and we never minded as long as the supporters behaved themselves. One day, the terraces around the pitch were completely deserted except for one character who was watching everything attentively.

I have always been a great believer in training players to improve their speed. The explosive change of pace is so important to footballers. I would mark out distances and have the lads sprinting in pairs against each other. This particular day I had my trainer standing at the far end to time the sprints, and I was at the start, telling the lads when to go. I had two of them lined up, tense, waiting for the word. I was making them hold on a bit, to get that explosiveness that is so vital. Suddenly this guy on the terraces shouted, 'Go!' and the lads shot off, then realised what had happened and stopped.

'Very bloody funny,' I shouted to this guy. 'You've had your fun. Now let us get on with our training.'

The lads were tensed up for a second time, waiting for my starting shout, when the guy went and did it again. 'Go!' he shouted, just as I was about to.

I was getting angry, while the lads were trying to hide their chuckles. 'Do that again,' I shouted to the guy, 'and you're out. It is not funny.'

So I got two more players tensed up and waiting. And he went and did it yet again!

This time I really lost my temper, and the lads were rolling around on the floor in helpless laughter. I could not see the funny side of it. Football, for me, has always been a serious business.

I went and called the police. 'Oh,' said the duty sergeant. 'That will be so-and-so. He's as mad as a March hare. He's obviously got out again.'

It turned out that he was the local nutcase whose favourite pastime was going around causing this sort of confusion. He was harmless enough, poor soul, but had completely disrupted the training session. I did not get any sense out of the players for the rest of the morning, and eventually I laughed so much about it that I had tears in my eyes.

Sir Bobby did not have the best of times with some fans when managing Ipswich. He got himself in trouble after Millwall hooligans had rioted during a 1970s match against his team. The FA warned him to watch his tongue after he said, 'These so-called fans are a disgrace. They should have turned the flame-throwers on them.'

Rangers and Celtic supporters would argue with some justification that they are the most devoted fans in the world. When Celtic became the first British club to win the European Cup in Lisbon in 1967 they carted much of the pitch home with them as souvenirs. The Portuguese police had never seen anything quite like the celebrating Celtic fans. They poured them on to special charter flights as fast as they could. A lot of them were flying higher than the planes. One of the supporters who had been herded on to an aircraft in a delirious condition sobered up somewhere above the North Sea when he realised he had *driven* out to Lisbon.

Supporters go to incredible lengths to show their allegiance. A Portsmouth fan has covered himself completely in the tattooed names of Fratton Park players, including – so rumour has it – someone called Shalop on his penis. Apparently, when he gets excited this becomes Shaka Hislop.

No doubt about the hungriest fan. Newcastle supporter Keith Roberts, who weighs in at a mere twenty-six stones, is famous at St James' Park for the NUFC initials hugely tattooed on one of his considerable bellies. Nicknamed Beefy, he gave his match-day menu to the Newcastle *Evening Chronicle*:

> *I get up early and have a full fry-up with all the trimmings. I keep myself going on the way to the match with a couple of cold saveloys and a nice steak pie. During the game you cannot beat the best football food of all, a tasty pasty. After that it's just rubbish – burgers, chicken wings, that sort of stuff. I make sure to leave room for the beer, of course. I always save the best for last – a lovely curry made by my wife when I get home. No match day is complete without it.*

I wonder how he and Delia Smith would get on?

Now here's what you call a really big football supporter. Jimmy Gardner, who rejoices in the nickname 'Five Bellies', gets a walk-on role alongside his best pal Paul Gascoigne in a 1997 charity game.

We've had the hungriest fan . . . and now for the angriest. A supporter in Brazil climbed up a tree that overlooked the Corinthians' ground, tied himself to it and said he would not come down until the Corinthians' manager changed the team's tactics. The club refused to give in to what they described as 'extortion' and the man was left up there for days, feeding off bananas thrown to him by passers-by. I reckon he was out of his tree.

Charlton Athletic sacked PA announcer Brian Cole for mocking the travelling Crystal Palace fans. He referred to the visitors as

'Crystal Palarse' and deliberately mispronounced Palace players' names.

Following complaints from Palace officials, Cole was relieved of his duties at half-time. He managed to say the word that is never on the lips of the likes of Tony Blair – 'sorry' – but it still didn't get him his job back. I think there must have been a humour bypass at the Valley.

Contrast that with Cardiff City's refusal to punish their match announcer for poking fun at West Ham fans. PA man Ali Yassine welcomed the Hammers to Ninian Park by playing what were described as 'a series of mickey-taking records' that included 'London Bridge is Falling Down', the theme from *Steptoe and Son* and Lonnie Donegan's rendition of 'My Old Man's a Dustman'. He also issued a request for 'the owner of a shire horse and rag-and-bone cart to return to his vehicle immediately'.

Yassine shrugged off accusations that his pre-match entertainment had been inflammatory. 'When has Lonnie Donegan ever been blamed for football hooliganism?' he retorted. West Ham officials, to their credit, saw the funny side. 'We don't have an issue with this,' said a Hammers spokesman. 'In fact, we find it quite amusing.'

If we forget how to laugh, we all might as well pack up and take the ball home.

The PA announcers are invariably mad-keen supporters of their clubs, and do the job for peanuts. Swindon Town's Peter Lewis famously criticised referee Graham Barber for sending off player–manager Steve McMahon. 'I've seen some crap refereeing decisions in my time, but that's the worst,' raged Lewis on air. On yer bike, Peter.

Another casualty of the killjoys was Celtic DJ 'Tiger' Tim Stevens, who lost his job after calling for a minute's silence at half-time 'in memory of Old Firm rivals, Rangers', who had just been knocked out of the European Cup by Levski Sofia.

Liverpool's PA man played 'Arrivederci Roma' during a Uefa Cup clash against Roma in February 2001. Italian officials and journalists were reportedly outraged but I thought it was hilarious. When did a little music and mirth hurt anybody?

'Fat Stan' Flashman, who was the king of the ticket touts – or, as he called himself, 'entertainment broker' – could get his hands on anything from a Buckingham Palace garden-party ticket to a seat at the Last Night of the Proms. But his richest harvest came from cup finals. He got his tickets on the old hush-hush from top players and managers who used to provide him with them under the counter in return for notes in the hand.

Back in 1971, he was in his King's Cross flat a couple of days after a Sunday newspaper had claimed that police were investigating his business. It was just before the Arsenal–Liverpool final in which the Gunners were going for the double. It was the hottest ticket in town, and Stan was in his element. He was checking through a wad of tickets he had been handed by his Highbury contacts when there was the sound of a police siren outside. He looked out of the window to see two police cars pulling up and four officers getting out, clearly intent on an arrest. 'They can't touch me without evidence,' Stan said to a pal as he started to flush the tickets down his toilet. There was a commotion outside Stan's front door, and then the police went off with a neighbour they had come to nab on a hit-and-run charge. They left behind a cursing and cussing Stan, with his arm down the loo seeing what he could retrieve. He later went 'legit' as the wildly eccentric chairman and owner of Barnet Football Club.

Diehard football fans can take their passions to the grave with a revolutionary new idea from an east London undertaker. The family firm offer personalised coffins painted in the colours of a client's favourite team. I wonder how long it will take for the money-hungry clubs to jump on the bandwagon – or the hearse –

and sell funeral kits. Perhaps Bury could sponsor them, and Gravesend would be the ideal place for the cemetery.

Surely one of the funniest chants ever was 'Robin Hood is gay, olé, olé'. This was sung by Dutch supporters of Feyenoord when they played Nottingham Forest. For some reason they thought it would annoy the Forest fans. But all they did was fall about laughing.

One of the weirdest chants I've heard from visiting fans at Anfield came when the Reds were playing West Ham off the park. By the time Liverpool had gone 4–0 clear the Hammers fans suddenly started jumping up and down and cheering. 'Let's pretend we've scored a goal, let's pretend we've scored a goal,' they chanted. Then they would cheer as if the ball had gone into the Liverpool net. They kept doing this until they seemed to have convinced themselves they were actually in the lead. The final score was Liverpool 5, West Ham 0. Maybe this was the start of fantasy football.

Leeds fans took an inflatable Spiderman and a blow-up sex doll to Elland Road, and were having fun pushing them back and forth in the air during a League match against Nottingham Forest. Then somebody had the idea of bringing them together to simulate sex, which was when stewards dived in and confiscated the dolls. The supporters, apparently, suddenly felt deflated.

How fanatical can you get? So they could watch the Euro 2000 championships without interruption from their wives or kids, two pals in Bristol locked themselves in a garden shed – fitted with a TV and with enough food and beer to get them through the tournament.

It reminds me of that great *Likely Lads* episode in which Terry and Bob went to enormous lengths not to hear the result of an England match that was being shown in a delayed recording that evening. They hid in locked rooms, wore earmuffs, refused to answer the phone or the door. After hours of ducking and diving they turned on the TV only to find the match had been fogged off. Priceless.

I did something similar once with a world heavyweight title fight. It was Frank Bruno against Tim Witherspoon. I dodged everybody so that I could watch the film of the fight without knowing the result. After managing to get to the programme time without knowing who won, I turned on the TV to hear the announcer say, 'And now to last night's fight and Frank Bruno's unsuccessful attempt to become world champion.' Like thousands of others, I almost smashed the set in anger. The announcer was soon knocked out of her job.

I am not sure I believe this one, but it's a great story. Man United season tickets were like gold dust after they had won the treble in the 1998–99 season. So nobody at the club could understand why one seat in the main stand was empty at every home game at the start of the following season. At last, for the Boxing Day game against Nottingham Forest, the seat was filled. A club steward approached the man sitting in the seat at half-time and said, 'Hope you don't mind me asking, but why have you not taken your seat for the previous games?'

'My wife bought it last summer,' the man explained. 'Then she hid it away as a surprise Christmas present.'

We have a flash character in Liverpool called Mark Roberts, who is obsessed with sharing all he has got with the world. He has made almost four hundred streaks at sporting events, and specialises in interrupting football matches. One of his classic exhibitions came during the 2002 Champions League final at Hampden Park, when he not only got on to the pitch bollock naked but managed to score with a shot into the Bayer Leverkusen net. He was arrested and fined two hundred pounds at Glasgow Sheriff's Court.

A Scottish FA spokesman said, 'He should have been given more than a slap on the wrist.' Where should he have been slapped then?

This deserves to be a 'What happened next?' poser *on A Question of Sport*. A streaker raced on to the pitch during the Cheshire Cup final between Witton Albion and Stockley Sports. Witton defender Brian Pritchard, an off-duty police constable, chased him and brought him down with a rugby tackle. Now, we freeze-frame the picture. What do you think happened next? I don't think you will quite believe the answer, but it's true. The referee sent off PC Pritchard for violent conduct! The decision was over-turned on appeal. Football my bare arse!

Continuing the unclothed theme, when that lovable rascal of a manager Malcolm Allison heard that seventies porn queen/writer Fiona Richmond was a Crystal Palace fan, he invited her to train with the team – topless, of course. Then, just to make it an even bigger splash for Fleet Street, he allowed her into the bath with the players. It made great publicity for the club ('Queen Shares Bath at the Palace'), and big trouble for the married players when they got home to their wives! Big Mal came out with the classic quote: 'Fiona lifted the dressing-room spirit when she climbed into the bath with us!' I bet that was not all she lifted.

You've gotta laugh

Gary Lineker was interviewing managers Steve Bruce and Sam Allardyce in a television show looking ahead to the new football season.

'So, Steve,' Gary says, 'what are your hopes for the coming season?'

Steve thinks carefully before answering: 'Well, provided we can pick up a few points in away games, I'm very confident that we can stay in the Premiership.'

Gary turns to Allardyce. 'Well, that's Steve's view. What about you, Sam? What are you predicting?'

'I have little doubt that we will walk away with the Premiership,' he says. 'We will at least reach the FA Cup final and the League Cup will be a doddle for us.'

'Er, don't you think you are exaggerating a bit there?' says an incredulous Lineker.

'Well, Steve started it,' says Sam.

Hark who's talking

Graeme Le Saux:
'He's started anticipating what's going to happen before it's even happened.'

Allan Clarke:
'I don't think, Brian. You don't think in this game.'

Peter Storey:
'Ah, the orgies, the birds, the booze and the fabulous money. Football was just a distraction.'

Michael Owen:
'It's great to get the first trophy under the bag.'

Charlie Nicholas:
'If sex ruined your game, all the married players would be out of a job.'

Roy Keane:
'If it's not the contract I want, then I won't sign it. That's not a threat.'

Paul Merson:
'The manager has given us unbelievable belief.'

John Terry:
'The manager could not even talk to us at half-time . . . He said we were bad.'

John Barnes:
'I just felt that the whole night, the conditions and taking everything into consideration, and everything being equal – and everything is equal – we should have got something from the game. But we didn't.'

David Platt:
'I couldn't really jet off to the States on a whim and a prayer.'

Chris Waddle:
'My legs sort of disappeared from nowhere.'

David Beckham:
'My parents have always been there for me, ever since I was about seven.'

Gary O'Neil:
'I was both surprised and delighted to take the armband for both legs.'

Ray Wilkins:
'We could be putting the hammer in Luton's coffin.'

Harry Kewell:
'I've always been a childhood Liverpool fan, even when I was a kid.'

Clinton Morrison:
'In the last ten minutes I was breathing out of my arse.'

Jonathan Woodgate:
'Leeds is a great club and it's been my home for years, even though I live in Middlesbrough.'

Ronnie Whelan:
'He's put on weight and I've lost it, and vice versa.'

Len Shackleton:
'The ball is round and should be kept rolling along like Old Father Tyne.'

Michael Hughes:
'The groin's been a bit sore, but after the semi-final I put it to the back of my head.'

Kenny Cunningham:
'I find the growing intervention by the football authorities in strictly footballing matters a rather worrying trend.'

Mo Johnston:
'If Rod Stewart can't pull the best-looking girls in the world, what chance have the rest of us got?'

Stan Bowles:
'If I had the choice of a night with Raquel Welch or going to a betting shop, I'd choose the betting shop.'

Vinnie Jones:
'If all else fails, you could wait for the first corner and tie Gullit's bleedin' dreadlocks to the goalpost.'

Martin Hodge:
'I spent four indifferent years at Goodison Park, but they were great.'

Bryan Robson:
'If we played like this every week, we wouldn't be so inconsistent.'

Jack Charlton:
'I have a little black book with the names of two players in it, and if I get the chance to do them I will. I'll make them suffer before I pack the game in. If I can kick them four yards over the touchline, believe me, I will.'

Terry McDermott:
'The best two clubs in London? Arsenal or Spurs? No way. Stringfellows and the Hippodrome.'

Bobby Moore:
'We were introduced to Sean Connery during a break in the 1966 World Cup finals, and Alf Ramsey kept calling him Seen. It was the funniest thing I've ever shawn or heard!'

11 The Things They Say

The Beautiful Game of football has developed into foot-and-mouth. With so much media exposure, we get almost as much entertainment from the things footballers say as from their performances on the pitch. Much of it is unintentionally hilarious in its content, and has brought us a whole new world of 'soccer speak'.

Mind you, there's nobody around today who can match the motormouth of a fifties and sixties player called Eddie Brown. He was an incredible character who used to shake hands with the corner flags, tell jokes to opponents during a match and, uniquely, could come up with a Shakespearean quote for every occasion. Lancastrian Eddie was a have-boots-will-travel centre-forward who banged in goals for his local club Preston before scoring for Southampton, Coventry, Birmingham – he was in their 1956 FA Cup final team – and Orient, and then for non-League clubs Scarborough, Bedworth and Wigan. He was brighter than your average footballer and later became a French teacher. Other players looked on open-mouthed as he would pick up the ball, hold it aloft and say, 'Alas poor Yorick, I knew him well . . . before we kicked the life out of him.' When making penalty claims, he would go on his knees and beg the referees to award the spot-kick. 'To be or not to be a penalty?' he would say, his hands clasped together. 'Out, damned spot! Out, I say!'

Come to think of it, that might have been more fitting coming from the mouth of David Beckham following his penalty misses against Turkey and Portugal.

Had Eddie Brown been playing today in this television age he would have been a mega personality. Imagine having a camera on him in the dressing-room as he made this call to arms to his team-mates before a match:

I see you stand like greyhounds in the slips,
Straining upon the start; The game's afoot:
Follow your spirit; and upon this charge
Cry 'God for Harry! England and Saint George!'

It sounds far fetched, but that is exactly what he used to do. How we could do with players brightening the after-match interviews in the Eddie Brown style rather than the cliché-cluttered rubbish many of them come out with these days. There have been so many footballers who have gone 'over the moon' or been 'as sick as a parrot' that it's a wonder there are any left fit to play the game.

But even Eddie Brown never came up with a quote like the following one, made by Claudio Ranieri, in an after-match Chelsea press conference that caused the mass collapse of the gathered reporters: 'Chelsea are my arse and I want my arse to cross the line first.'

Fleet Street's finest looked at him with open mouths. 'Er, your *arse*, Claudio?'

He looked puzzled, muttered quietly with the interpreter who had been helping him improve his English, and then laughed out loud.

'Gentlemen, I make big mistake,' he said. 'No, not my arse – my *horse*!'

Another Italian, Paolo di Canio, showed the all-round grasp of language needed at Premiership clubs these days when he arrived at a Charlton training session with the United Nations greetings:

'*Buon giorno . . . guten Morgen . . . bonjour . . . buonas díaz . . .* lovely jubbly!'

Here's a corker courtesy of Midlands anecdote collector Ian Allen.

'Have you heard of Kenny Burns?' he asked.

'Of course I have,' I said. 'Nottingham Forest and Scotland defender.'

'How about Tommy Burns?' he asked.

'Celtic player and former manager,' I replied.

'Correct,' he said. 'Do you know Vic Burns?'

'No,' I replied.

'Well,' he said, 'it does if you rub it on your bollocks.'

Continuing with the not-quite-football stories, how about this one from Terry Venables:

> *I was a young apprentice at Chelsea when the manager, Ted Drake, offered me a lift after a game. Ted could talk until the cows came home and I listened respectfully as he rabbited on and on about the good old days. Then he got wrapped up in talking about his concerns about the current first team. He lost all concentration on his driving at this point, and we sat at traffic lights while he went on and on. The lights changed twice and the drivers behind started going mad with their horns. Suddenly Ted stopped talking, looked across at me as if he was seeing me for the first time and then looked behind him. 'Bloody hell,' he said in his Hampshire burr, 'I thought you were driving.'*

It was a loss to the quotes factory when Gordon Strachan took a break from the managing game, and it was great to see him back in business with Celtic. He is a genuinely funny man, and many of his comments are wisecracks that top comedy scriptwriters would find hard to match. You are never quite sure when he is being serious because he will make his comments behind a poker face, a bit like his fellow Scot Chic Murray used to deliver his wonderful material. For example, he may have been pulling legs when he said after a defeat: 'I tried to get the disappointment out of my system by going for a walk. I ended up seventeen miles from home and I had to phone my wife to come and pick me up.'

But the modern manager who provides quote collectors with most laughs, although in his case often involuntarily, is one of my favourite footballers of all time, Kevin Keegan. He came out with this pearl after a referee had been quick on the draw with name-taking: 'The ref's shirt pocket is like a toaster. Every time there's a tackle, up pops a yellow card.'

The quotes running through this book have been collected in partnership with my pal, sports historian Norman Giller, the Judge of the *Sun*. He has been collecting and collating sports quotes since compiling a 'Quote Unquote' column back in the

No, it's not Bill and Ben the Flowerpot Men. Here are two of England's future managers photographed in their playing days: Kevin Keegan and Glenn Hoddle. Kev is saying, 'Wonder how we'll manage, Hod?' 'We'll be all right,' says Hoddle. 'We behaved ourselves in our previous lives.'

days of the *Daily Herald* before it was transformed into the *Sun*. We voted the following our favourites . . .

Paddy Crerand:
'Sir Matt always believed Manchester United would be one of the greatest clubs in the world. He was the eternal optimist. In 1968, he still hoped Glenn Miller was just missing.'

George Best:
'I once said Gazza's IQ was less than his shirt number, and he asked me, "What's an IQ?"'

Craig Brown:
'When I joined Rangers I immediately established myself as third-choice left-half. The guys ahead of me were an amputee and a Catholic.'

Jimmy Hagan *(when Vitoria Setubal manager)*:
'I shouldn't be too upset at losing to Benfica. After all, they have the best players, the best referees and the best linesmen.'

Danny Blanchflower:
'The FA Cup final is a great occasion until ten minutes before the kick-off. Then the players come on and ruin the whole thing.'

Harry Redknapp:
'That Dani is so good looking I don't know whether to pick him or f*** him!'

David Beckham:
'I definitely want Brooklyn to be christened, but I don't know into what religion yet.'

Jim Baxter:
'When Charlie Cooke sold defenders a dummy, they had to pay to get back into the ground.'

Brian Clough:
'Trevor Brooking floats like a butterfly, and he stings like one, too.'

Archie Gemmill:
'If Graeme Souness was a bar of chocolate, he'd eat himself.'

Karren Brady *(before she married a footballer)*:
'Footballers are only interested in drinking, clothes and the size of their willies.'

Phil Woosnam:
'The rules of soccer are very simple. Basically it is this: if it moves, kick it; if it doesn't move, kick it until it does.'

Giovanni Trapattoni:
'The chances of Paolo di Canio playing for Italy while I am in charge? Only if there's an outbreak of bubonic plague.'

Kevin Keegan:
'That would have been a goal if the goalkeeper hadn't saved it.'

Joe Mercer:
'If only Stan Bowles could pass a betting shop like he passes a ball.'

Jasper Carrott:
'I hear Glenn Hoddle has found God. That must have been one hell of a pass.'

Garth Crooks:
'Football is football. If that weren't the case it wouldn't be the game that it is.'

Steve Coppell:
'Glen Little dropped out shortly before the kick-off because he had tweaked a hamstring walking upstairs at home. We're now asking him to move to a bungalow.'

Jimmy Greaves:
'Would you Adam and Eve it. We've had cocaine, bribery and Arsenal scoring two goals at home. But just when you thought there were no surprises left in football, Vinnie Jones turns out to be an international player.'

Gary Megson:
'Let's just say this player is not blessed with the greatest intelligence. He spelled his name wrong on his transfer request.'

Terry Venables:
'I felt a lump in my throat as the ball went in.'

David Pleat:
'Maradona gets tremendous elevation with his balls, no matter what position he's in.'

Jack Charlton:
'It was a game we should have won. We lost it because we thought we were going to win it. But then again, I thought that there was no way we were going to get a result there.'

Craig Bellamy:
'Arsenal are streets ahead of everyone in the Premiership, and Man United are up there with them.'

Claudio Ranieri:
'If you need just a first eleven and four others, why did Columbus sail to India to discover America?'

Theo Foley:
'If you had to name one particular person to blame, it would have to be the players.'

Carlton Palmer:
'Vinnie Jones, Dennis Wise and John Fashanu must be turning in their graves over what's happening at Wimbledon.'

Kevin Keegan:
'I know what's around the corner – I just don't know where the corner is. But the onus is on us to perform and we must control the bandwagon.'

Lawrie McMenemy:
'When you're 4–0 up you should never lose 7–1.'

Ian Rush:
'Djimi Traore had to adapt to the English game, and he did that by going out on loan to Lens last season.'

Keith Burkinshaw:
'Ossie Ardiles puts his finger on it when he says: "If you're confident, you're always totally different to the player that's lacking confidence." Ossie is a trained lawyer, y'know.'

John Bond:
'His strengths were my weaknesses, and my weaknesses were his strengths.'

Dave Bassett:
'Obviously, for Scunthorpe it would be nice to be able to put Wimbledon on their bottoms.'

Mike England:
'Ian Rush is perfectly fit, apart, that is, from his physical fitness.'

Craig Brown:
'The underdogs will start favourites for this match.'

Lawrie McMenemy:
'Stan Mortensen was the last player to score a hat-trick in an FA Cup final. He even had a final named after him – the Matthews final.'

Robbie Savage:
'I'm not Pele or Maradona.'

There was never any chance of Britain's first million-pound footballer Trevor Francis getting too big for his boots.

Kevin Keegan:
'There's nobody bigger or smaller than Maradona.'

Paul Gascoigne:
'Because of the booking I will miss the Holland game – if I'm selected.'

Sir Bobby Robson:
'He's very fast. If he gets a yard ahead of himself nobody will catch him.'

John Hollins:
'A contract on a piece of paper, saying you want to leave, is like a piece of paper saying you want to leave.'

Terry Venables:
'If you can't stand the heat of the dressing-room, get out of the kitchen.'

John Greig:
'Football's not like an electric light. You can't just flick the switch and change from quick to slow.'

Steve Coppell:
'I'm not going to make it a target, but it is something to aim for.'

Ruud Gullit:
'We must have had 99 per cent of the game. It was the other 3 per cent that cost us the match.'

Sir Alex Ferguson:
'The philosophy of a lot of European teams, even in home matches, is not to give a goal away.'

Glenn Hoddle:
'When a player gets to thirty, so does his body.'

 You've gotta laugh

The trial of Saddam Hussein in Iraq draws to a close and he is found guilty and sentenced to be shot at dawn.

The judge tells the fallen dictator, 'The one wish we will grant you is that you can choose the person who will do the shooting.'

Without hesitation, Saddam says, 'David Beckham from twelve yards.'

12 Do Not Adjust Your Set

As somebody who spends a lot of my time spouting off on the box, I should be careful about taking the mic out of any broadcaster who gets caught with his foot in his mouth. I am the man who infamously managed to make a spoonerism of 'a cunning stunt', and held up production on *Down to Earth* because nobody could keep a straight face when I kept messing up the line 'It's my turn to pluck the flipping turkey.'

So the managers, commentators, studio experts and full cast of footballers I am quoting in this chapter have my sympathy for getting caught out at the microphone. It has become almost a national game to spot their trips of the tongue, with the pee-taking pot stirred for years by the 'Colemanballs' column in *Private Eye* magazine.

David Coleman, of course, was the master of the on-camera cock-up. But let's be fair to him, he did more live television broadcasts than almost anybody else on earth, and that meant he was like a tightrope-walker working without a safety-net. Coleman had a vast knowledge of all sports, and was so keen to share his knowledge with the viewers that he often talked before his brain was properly in gear.

Let me share just a few of his classic gaffes with you, and you will understand why he inspired the magazine column:

Referring to Asa Hartford, who had just been revealed as

having a hole in his heart, Coleman said during a match commentary, 'He is a wholehearted player . . .'

He was about to introduce highlights of an international match and said, 'Don't tell anybody coming in now the result of that fantastic match. Now let's have another look at Italy's winning goal.'

Anchoring *Grandstand*, he used to stand by the ticker-tape machine in the pre-computer results days and was brilliant at firing facts off the top of his head. But sometimes it came out as nonsense: 'Nottingham Forest are having a bad run . . . They've lost six matches now without winning.'

Coleman was at Wembley for the FA Cup final in 1973. 'On this hundred and first FA Cup final day,' he said, 'there are just two teams left.'

During a match commentary, he shared the thought: 'If that had gone in, it would have been a goal.'

I wonder how many puzzled faces there were among viewers when he told them, 'For those of you watching who do not have television sets, there is live commentary on Radio Two.'

And a last classic from the master that no doubt put years on him: 'He's thirty-one this year; last year he was thirty.'

So David Coleman set the standard, but John Motson matched him with this all-time gem: 'For those of you watching in black and white, Tottenham are wearing the yellow shirts.' Marvellous, Motty!

And I would have loved to see the screen debut of Bob Wilson at the start of what became a distinguished broadcasting career. He was still a goalkeeper with Arsenal when the BBC tested him, asking him to give news of Highbury team changes to camera. Our Bob came hot-foot from the dressing-room, and breathlessly told the nation, 'Charlie George has just pissed a late fartness test.'

On with the collection. Do not adjust your sets . . .

Commentators at the Mic

John Motson:
'The Argentinians are numbered alphabetically.'

Barry Davies:
'The Austrians are wearing the dark black socks.'

Rob Hawthorne:
'All of West Ham's away victories have come on opponents' territory.'

John Helm:
'We're coming to the end of the half, and the referee is looking at his whistle.'

Gerry Harrison:
'Larosa is nineteen – that's on his back, that is.'

Alan Parry:
'With the last kick of the game, Macdonald has scored with a header.'

Clive Tyldesley:
'He's not George Best, but then again, no one is.'

George Hamilton:
'Welcome to the Nou Camp Stadium in Barcelona that is packed to capacity . . . with some patches of seats left empty.'

David Coleman:
'The pace of this match is really accelerating, by which I mean it is getting faster all the time.'

Martin Tyler:
'McCarthy shakes his head in agreement with the referee.'

Ron Atkinson (as Steve McManaman hoisted the European Cup after helping Real Madrid beat Valencia):
'You won't see that again now that the Scouser's got it.'

Andy Gray:
'There was no contact there – just a clash of bodies.'

John Motson:
'Reinders is standing on the ball with Breitner, and Müller has gone to join them.'

Barry Davies:
'He must be feeling on cloud seven.'

Ian Darke:
'And with just four minutes gone, the score is already 0–0.'

Ron Atkinson:
'I'm going to make a prediction – it could go either way.'

John Helm:
'Such a positive move by Uruguay – bringing two players off and putting two players on.'

Martin Tyler:
'The ageless Dennis Wise, now in his thirties.'

George Hamilton:
'He's pulling him off! The manager is pulling his captain off.'

Alan Parry:
'And Ritchie has now scored eleven goals, exactly double the number he scored last season.'

John Helm:
'The USA are a goal down, and if they don't get a goal, they'll lose.'

Barry Davies:
'The crowd think that Todd handled the ball. They must have seen something that nobody else did.'

Brian Moore *(at the final whistle, which signalled Nottingham Forest had beaten Hamburg)*:
'And Hamburg have won the European Cup!'

John Motson:
'The World Cup – truly an international event.'

TV Presenters at the Mic

Des Lynam:
'Real's second goal made it 3–0.'

Jim Rosenthal:
'We can't tell you the result, but the winning goal from Niall Quinn was his fourteenth of the season.'

230

Jeff Stelling:
'Chris Porter scored his first League goal last week, and he's done the same this week.'

Jimmy Hill:
'Scotland were unlucky not to get another penalty like the one that wasn't given in the first half.'

Gary Newbon:
'There's such a fine line between defeat and losing.'

Steve Rider:
'If you don't want to know the result, look away now as we show you Tony Adams lifting the trophy.'

Des Lynam:
'He kicked wide of the goal with such precision.'

Fred Dinenage:
'There is no change in the top six, except that Leeds United have moved into the top six.'

Jimmy Greaves:
'The only thing that Norwich didn't get was the goal that they finally got.'

David Coleman:
'The Italians are hoping for an Italian victory.'

Frank Bough:
'The Norwich goal was scored by Kevin Bond, who is the son of his father.'

Jimmy Sanderson:
'I predicted in August that Celtic would reach the final. Now, on the eve of the final, I stand by that prediction.'

Matthew Lorenzo:
'Forest scored after twenty-two seconds – totally against the run of play.'

Jim Rosenthal:
'Peter Ward has become a new man – just like his old self.'

Des Lynam:
'There's a simple recipe about this sports business. If you're a sporting star, you're a sporting star. If you don't quite make it, you become a coach. If you can't coach, you become a journalist. If you can't spell, you introduce *Grandstand* on a Saturday afternoon.'

My pal Al. I had shaved off my beard for a part I was playing when I appeared with Ally McCoist on *A Question of Sport.* The bitingly witty Scot said, 'Without your beard, Ricky, your face looks like my arse . . . my arse!'

Experts at the Mic

Ally McCoist:
'Real Madrid are probably, without doubt, the best team in the world.'

Mark Lawrenson:
'Ireland will give 99 per cent – everything they've got.'

Chris Kamara:
'It's real end-to-end stuff . . . but unfortunately it's all up at Forest's end.'

Alan McInally:
'In any walk of life, if you get a penalty, you expect to score.'

Lawrie McMenemy:
'I hope Robson doesn't blow up because of the heat.'

Kevin Keegan:
'I want more from David Beckham. I want him to improve on perfection.'

Sir Bobby Robson:
'We're taking twenty-two players to Italy, sorry, to Spain . . . Where are we, Jim?'

Ian Wright:
'Without being too harsh on David Beckham, he cost us the match.'

Mike Channon:
'Kenny Dalglish has about as much personality as a tennis racket.'

Andy Gray:
'Anyone who takes drugs should be hammered.'

Jimmy Greaves:
'One word sums up that performance – a total humiliating mess.'

Peter Schmeichel:
'Solskjaer never misses the target. That time he hit the post.'

Trevor Steven:
'Brian Laudrup wasn't facing just one defender – he was facing one at the front and one at the back as well.'

Barry Venison:
'The Croatians don't play well without the ball.'

Mark Lawenson:
'If Plan A fails, they could always revert to Plan A.'

Ian St John:
'Batistuta gets most of his goals with the ball.'

Dave Bassett:
'An inch or two either side of the post and that would have been a goal.'

Sir Alex Ferguson:
'It's a conflict of parallels.'

Kevin Keegan:
'The game has gone rather scrappy as both sides realise they could win this match or lose it.'

Ian Wright:
'The referee was booking everyone. I thought he was filling in his lottery numbers.'

Chris Kamara:
'Robert Earnshaw has scored goals in the Nationwide. That proves he's a Premiership player.'

Rodney Marsh:
'I'm not going to pick out anyone in particular, but Jay-Jay Okocha should not be the captain of a football club.'

John Gidman:
'They have got their feet on the ground, and if they stay that way they will go places.'

John Greig:
'Celtic manager Davie Hay still has a fresh pair of legs up his sleeve.'

Robbie Earle:
'If you're 0–0 down, there's no one better to get you back on terms than Ian Wright.'

Jack Charlton:
'The players with the wind will have to control it more.'

Gordon Taylor:
'The FA's priority seems to be having a good national stadium at Wembley rather than a good team to play in it.'

George Best:
'I'd have to be Superman to do some of the things I'm supposed to have done. I've often been in six different places at six different times.'

Jimmy Greaves:
'Kevin Keegan was not fit to lace George Best's boots – or his drinks.'

David Pleat:
'He had to cut back inside on to his left because he hasn't got a right foot.'

Joe Royle:
'Wolves beat Palace convincingly without being convincing.'

Chris Kamara:
'For Burnley to win, they are going to have to score.'

Derek Dougan:
'People keep talking about total football. All I know about is Total petrol.'

Kevin Keegan:
'He opened his legs and went pretty quick.'

At the Radio Mic

Alan Green:
'You don't score sixty-four goals in eighty-six games without being able to score goals.'

Mike Ingham:
'Tottenham are trying tonight to become the first London team to win this cup. The last team to do it was the 1973 Spurs side.'

Alan Brazil:
'Our talking point this morning is George Best, his liver transplant and the booze culture in football. Don't forget, the best caller wins a crate of John Smith's.'

Stuart Hall:
'What will you do when you leave football, Jack? Will you stay in football?'

Jason Cundy:
'Iain Dowie knows that points dropped at home are points dropped.'

Brian Marwood:
'There's still forty-five minutes to go – for both sides, I would guess.'

Mike Ingham:
'Neil Sullivan has stopped absolutely everything United have thrown at him and it's Wimbledon 1, Manchester United 1.'

Bryon Butler:
'The reason Johnny Giles is dominating in midfield is that he caresses his balls rather than just thumping them.'

Jimmy Armfield:
'I think they should have left Tony Morley on as a down-and-out winger.'

Peter Withe:
'Both sides have scored a couple of goals, and both sides have conceded a couple of goals.'

Anonymous:
'Julian Dicks is everywhere. It's like they've got eleven Dicks on the pitch.'

Eamonn Andrews:
'And here in the *Sports Report* studio I am delighted to welcome one of the legendary figures of football, a name on everybody's lips . . . um, except mine . . . I'm sorry, please excuse me . . . it has completely slipped my

memory. [It was Sir Stanley Rous, who – with a chuckle – introduced himself.]'

Brian Marwood:
'That's twice now that Terry Phelan has got between himself and the goal.'

Mark Bright:
'The crowd will be looking for Vieri to inspirate them.'

Radio 5 goal flash:
'Emile Zola has scored again for Chelsea.'

Another Radio 5 goal flash:
'It's now 1–1, an exact reversal of the scoreline on Saturday.'

Mike Parry:
'David Beckham's wife appears to be no different from five million other girls, but she's got something that sets her apart from the other four million, nine hundred and fifty thousand and ninety-five.'

Lawrie Sanchez:
'Bolton are literally encamped on the edge of the box.'

Steve Coppell:
'The lad got overexcited when he saw the white of the goalpost's eyes.'

Anonymous newsreader:
'He is noted for being a snoring winger. I'm sorry, that should be a scoring winger.'

Alan Green:
'This will be their nineteenth consecutive game without a win unless they can get an equaliser.'

Jimmy Armfield:
'With eight minutes left, the game could be won or lost in the next five or ten minutes.'

Derek Rae:
'It's headed away by John Clark, using his head.'

Tommy Docherty:
'Robert Maxwell tried to buy Brighton and Hove Albion, but pulled out when he discovered it was only one club.'

Gerry Francis:
'What I said to them at half-time would be unprintable on the radio.'

Mike Ingham:
'Martin O'Neill, standing, hands on hips, stroking his chin.'

Eamonn Andrews:
'I'm just hearing in my headphones that Bobby Charlton has scored an equaliser against Manchester United . . . Hold on, that can't be right . . . Sorry, that should be Charlton Athletic have equalised against Manchester United . . . Sorry, that should be Charlton has scored against Charlton. Oh dear, a case of too many Charltons spoiling the broth.'

Denis Law:
'Whoever wins today will win the championship no matter who wins.'

Trevor Brooking:
'That's football, Mike. Northern Ireland have had several chances and haven't scored but England have had no chances and have scored twice.'

Total Bollocks at the Mic

George Graham:
'If Liverpool finish sixth and you get more points than them, you're looking at finishing fifth. Or even fourth.'

Alan Smith:
'I'd love to be a fly on the Panathinaikos dressing-room wall – if I could speak Greece.'

Ron Atkinson:
'He sliced the ball when he had it on a plate.'

Barry Davies:
'Lukic saved with his foot, which is all part of the goalkeeper's arm.'

David Pleat:
'Eighty per cent of teams who score first in matches go on to win them. But they may draw some. Or occasionally lose.'

Fabien Barthez:
'Unconsciously, I fell in love with the small round sphere with its amusing and capricious rebounds which sometimes play with me.'

Trevor Brooking:
'That could have been his second yellow card – if he'd already got his first one, of course.'

Glenn Hoddle:
'About seventy-five per cent of what happens to Paul Gascoigne in his life is fiction.'

John Docherty:
'Chester made it hard for us by having two players sent off.'

Peter Beardsley:
'Two–nil was a dangerous lead to have.'

Anonymous:
'For f***'s sake, we're on air in a minute.'

Graeme Souness:
'Today's top players only want to play in London or for Manchester United. That's what happened when I tried to sign Alan Shearer and he went to Blackburn.'

Sir Alex Ferguson:
'This pilot move by FIFA will take root and fly.'

Paul Elliott:
'He'd no alternative but to make a needless tackle.'

Kevin Keegan:
'He can't speak Turkey, but you can tell he's delighted.'

Lennie Lawrence:
'What he's got is legs, which the other midfielders don't have.'

Alan Ball:
'The important thing is he shook hands with us over the phone.'

Ron Greenwood:
'Playing with wingers is more effective against European teams like Brazil than English sides like Wales.'

Glenn Hoddle:
'At international level, players should be able to handle the ball.'

John Motson:
'And I suppose Spurs are now nearer to being out of the FA Cup than at any other time since the first half of this season, when they weren't ever in it anyway.'

Brian Kidd:
'We pressed the self-destruct button ourselves.'

Andy Gray:
'The most vulnerable area for goalies is between their legs.'

Denis Law:
'The advantage of being at home is very much with the home side.'

Kevin Keegan:
'I came to Nantes two years ago and it is much the same today, except that it's completely different.'

Gerald Sinstadt:
'I'm sure that Ron Greenwood will hope that by the time England go to Spain Kevin Keegan has got his misses out of his system.'

Ian St John:
'I wouldn't be surprised if this game went all the way to the finish.'

John Bond:
'I have other irons in the fire, but I am keeping them close to my chest.'

Archie McPherson:
'There aren't many last chances left for George Best.'

George Gavin:
'So this film you're starring in, *The George Best Story*. Tell us what it's about.'

Alan Green:
'It was the game that put the Everton ship back on the road.'

Alex Ferguson:
'The lads really ran their socks into the ground.'

Phil Neal:
'When England go to Turkey there could be fatalities – or even worse, injuries.'

David Coleman:
'Peru score their third, and it's 3–1 to Scotland.'

John Helm:
'West Germany's Briegel hasn't been able to get past anyone yet – that's his trademark.'

Sir Bobby Robson:
'Tottenham have impressed me. They haven't thrown in the towel even though they've been under the gun.'

Alan Parry:
'He'll probably wake up having sleepless nights about that one.'

Jimmy Hill:
'Graham Rix was not so much off-colour as not quite on song.'

Anonymous:
'So United have not been able to improve on their one hundred per cent record.'

Alan Shearer:
'You only get one opportunity of an England debut.'

David Beckham:
'That was in the past – we're in the future now.'

Terry Venables:
'Apart from their goals, Norway haven't scored.'

Chris Cattlin:
'There's a rat in the camp throwing a spanner in the works.'

Nobody has had a fuller football life than Jimmy Hill – footballer, coach, manager, PFA chairman, pioneering TV pundit, Fulham chairman … and linesman. Because he was a qualified referee, Jimmy ran the line following an injury to an official in a League game at Highbury. I know a few people in the game who would like to tell him where to stick that flag. Football my arse!

Ron Greenwood:
'They have missed so many chances they must be wringing their heads in shame.'

Paul Ince:
'We have to be careful not to let our game not be the game we know it should be.'

Alan Shearer:
'There's no way the future is over for the likes of Martin Keown, Tony Adams and David Seaman.'

Barry Davies:
'Poland nil, England nil, though England are now looking the better value for their nil.'

Archie McPherson:
'Johan Cruyff at the age of thirty-five added a whole new meaning to the word Anno Domini.'

Eamonn Andrews:
'We're now going to Wembley for live second-half commentary on the England–Scotland game, um, except that it's at Hampden Park.'

Michael Owen:
'I was both surprised and delighted when the FA knocked on my doorbell.'

David Coleman:
'Manchester United are buzzing around the goalmouth like red bluebottles.'

Jimmy Hill:
'It is a cup final, and the one that wins it goes through.'

Niall Quinn:
'He managed to make a good hash of it in the end.'

David Beckham:
'Alex Ferguson is the best manager I've ever had at this level. Well, he's the only manager I've actually had at this level. But he's the best manager I've ever had.'

Ron Greenwood:
'Being given chances – and not taking them. That's what life's all about.'

Ron Atkinson:
'He dribbles a lot and the opposition don't like it – you can see it all over their faces.'

Jack Charlton:
'If in winning we only draw we would be fine.'

Trevor Brooking:
'Being naturally right-footed, he doesn't often chance his arm with his left foot.'

Gary Newbon:
'And there'll be more football in a moment, but first we've got the highlights of the Scottish League Cup final.'

Jimmy Greaves:
'Well, Brian, I've watched every kick, every tackle, every pass and every shot of this World Cup. It has all been about balls – long balls, short balls, square balls, through balls, high balls, dipping balls, trapped balls, headed balls, netted balls. In fact, it has been a load of balls.'

And, finally, the last word has to go to the master, David Coleman, when introducing *Match of the Day* immediately after a cooking show featuring Fanny Craddock:

'And for those of you who watched the last programme, I hope all your doughnuts turn out like Fanny's.'

You've gotta laugh

Harry Redknapp is getting concerned about Southampton's loss of form and he decides to telephone Alex Ferguson for some advice.

'Sir Alex,' he says, 'you're one of the most successful managers in the history of the game. What's your secret?'

'Cones, Harry,' Sir Alex replies. 'Cones.'

'Cones?' says Harry. 'What does that mean?"

'Every day in training,' explains Sir Alex, 'all the United players dribble footballs around traffic cones that I line up in different formations depending on the team we are meeting in the next match – 4–4–2, 4–3–3, you know the sort of thing.'

'And you think that will help me?' says Harry.

'Well, it's worked for me,' says Sir Alex. 'Give it a go, and let me know how your players get on with it. Just wait and see how it improves their ball control and sharpness.'

Harry puts down the telephone, and as he thinks through the advice from Sir Alex he realises he should have asked another question.

He dials the Man United office again and says, 'What about my goalkeeper, Sir Alex? Do I play him, too?'

'Of course,' says Sir Alex. 'Your defenders can practise passing back to him, and he can sharpen up his throwing and kicking.'

'Good point, Sir Alex. You're the main man.'

Two weeks later Sir Alex has heard no more. Curiosity gets the better of him and he telephones Harry.

'Hello, Sir Alex,' says Harry, with a heavy, sad voice.

'What's the matter?' asks Sir Alex. 'You sound so depressed.'

'It's the cones, Sir Alex,' says Harry. 'The cones.'

'The cones? What about the cones?'

Harry takes a deep breath and says, 'They effing-well beat us 3–0.'

'How on earth did that happen?' asks a disbelieving Sir Alex.

'My bloody goalkeeper', says Harry, 'let in three own goals.'

Other bestselling titles available by mail

☐ Ricky   Ricky Tomlinson £6.99

☐ Cheers My Arse!   Ricky Tomlinson £6.99

☐ Reading My Arse!   Ricky Tomlinson £1.99

The prices shown above are correct at time of going to press. However, the publishers reserve the right to increase prices on covers from those previously advertised, without further notice.

───────────────── sphere ─────────────────

Please allow for postage and packing: **Free UK delivery.**
Europe: add 25% of retail price; Rest of World: 45% of retail price.

To order any of the above or any other Sphere titles, please call our credit card orderline or fill in this coupon and send/fax it to:

Sphere, PO Box 121, Kettering, Northants NN14 4ZQ
Fax: 01832 733076 Tel: 01832 737526
Email: aspenhouse@FSBDial.co.uk

☐ I enclose a UK bank cheque made payable to Sphere for £ . . . .
☐ Please charge £ . . . . . . to my Visa/Delta/Maestro

Expiry Date [ ][ ][ ][ ] Maestro Issue No. [ ][ ]

NAME (BLOCK LETTERS please) . . . .

ADDRESS . . . .

. . . .

. . . .

Postcode . . . . Telephone . . . .

Signature . . . .

Please allow 28 days for delivery within the UK. Offer subject to price and availability.